SpringerBriefs in Political Science

More information about this series at http://www.springer.com/series/8871

Peter Emerson

Democratic Decision-making

Consensus Voting for Civic Society and Parliaments

Springer

Peter Emerson
The de Borda Institute
Belfast, UK

ISSN 2191-5466 ISSN 2191-5474 (electronic)
SpringerBriefs in Political Science
ISBN 978-3-030-52807-2 ISBN 978-3-030-52808-9 (eBook)
https://doi.org/10.1007/978-3-030-52808-9

This Springer imprint is published by the registered company Springer Nature Switzerland AG
The registered company address is: Gewerbestrasse 11, 6330 Cham, Switzerland

To the victims of majoritarianism, everywhere;[1] *and not least to...*

the 40 millions who died in Máo Zédōng's anti-rightist campaign and its consequent famine;
the 20 million + who suffered under bolshevism[2] *in Lenin's and then Stalin's gulags;*
the almost one million who were slaughtered in the genocide in Rwanda;[3]
the many thousands who died in the Balkans[4] *and...*
the Caucasus of the 1990s;
the 3000 who were killed in 'the Troubles' in Northern Ireland;
and
the similar number who were murdered in Kenya after the 2007 elections.

[1]I mention only the conflicts of those countries in which I have travelled if not sojourned, and whose politics I have studied.

[2]The very word 'bolshevism' means 'majoritarianism'.

[3]The *Interahamwe* launched their murderous campaign with the slogan, '*Rubanda nyamwinshi*'—'we are the majority'.

[4]'All the wars in the former Yugoslavia started with a referendum'. (*Oslobodjenje*, 7.2.1999—author's translation.)

Foreword

The theory of voting and its formal foundation, the social choice theory, is shot through with negative results typically framed as incompatibilities of conditions thought to be plausible or even essential for democratic decision-making in groups. The best-known of such results is Arrow's impossibility theorem that some seventy years ago set the stage for a voluminous literature on conditions that one could impose on reasonable voting rules. Quite a few such desiderata have been defined, analysed and shown to be mutually incompatible. The main upshot, it is often maintained, is then that no ideal voting rule exists. Therefore, one has to pick one's favourite from a set of rules that all have at least one serious flaw.

In the course of these studies, two camps of voting theorists have emerged: (i) those emphasising pairwise majority comparisons and (ii) those focusing on the positions of candidates in voter preferences in determining the winning candidates. For a long time, the former camp seemed to have the upper hand in the contest between these two if for no other reason than the intuitive idea that the majority rule seems to capture the essence of democratic decision-making. And indeed, it makes sense to argue that the majority rule is more democratic than the minority rule in the sense a larger number of people get their way than in the case the minority view would prevail.

This argument loses its intuitive appeal in settings where a small minority has a very strong preference for the losing option, while most members of the majority are nearly indifferent on the issue but lean ever so slightly towards the winning option. Perhaps a theoretically more serious weakness of the argument pertains to the fundamental ambiguity of the majority winner. This is blatantly obvious in voting contexts where more than two alternatives are on the agenda, but the ambiguity may present itself in the two alternative cases as well. This is illustrated in the referendum paradox.

Suppose that a consultative referendum involving two options, say opt-in to or opt-out from a union of states, is arranged in a country where there are—for simplicity of the argument—just three provinces or districts each with ten million voters. Suppose that the opinions of the voters are distributed so that in provinces 1 and 2, a clear majority of six million vs. four million prefers opt-out to opt-in, whereas in province 3 all ten million voters prefer opt-in. Each province sends one representative to the parliament, where the issue is to be finally decided. Now, the MPs from districts 1 and 2 should, if they wish to reflect the views of the majority of their province, vote for opt-out. *A fortiori*, the MP from district 3 should vote for opt-in. So, in the parliamentary vote, the outcome is 2 to 1 for opt-out. The popular vote, in contrast, would lead to the victory of opt-in with a 18 million–12 million margin. So, which outcome is the majority one?

The ambiguity of the majority decision is even more transparent in some settings involving more than two alternatives or candidates. To illustrate, consider a setting involving three options: x, y and z along with the distribution of nine million voters into three opinion groups so that four million prefer x to z to y, three million prefer y to z to x and two million prefer z to y to x. Supposing that each voter votes according to his/her preferences, x wins the first-past-the-post contest with four million votes. It is thus the plurality winner. One could argue that the plurality winner be elected in this case since its number of votes is larger than that of any other alternative. Suppose, however, that—since x did not garner a majority (but just a plurality) of votes—a plurality run-off contest is arranged between the two largest vote-getters x and y. In the run-off, one can expect y to win, since those two million voters whose favourite is not present in the run-off contest prefer y to x. Hence, the former gets five million and the latter four million votes. Thus, y is the majority winner. So, we have now two winners out of three depending on how we interpret the notion of majority. However, the strongest case can be built for arguing that z is the true majority winner. This argument is based on the fact that z would win both x and y—that is, all its competitors—in separate majority comparisons, the former with a five million—four million and the latter with a six million—three million margin. So, depending on our definition of the majority winner each one of the three alternatives can be regarded as the winner in the example.

The ambiguity is, however, not the only—or even the main—reason Peter Emerson rejects the majoritarian view as the guiding principle of institutional design. He deems the view as downright dangerous because of its built-in tendency to evoke conflicts and to exacerbate cleavages in societies. His many travels in conflict-ridden parts of the world have inspired him to thinking about alternative ways of teasing out the will of the people in referendum-like situations. On the basis of his first-hand experience and theoretical literature, he also proposes and evaluates methods of parliamentary elections as well as of making collective choices in the day-to-day business of government and/or of other types of assemblies.

The basic motivation of the book, conflict avoidance or mitigation, is at the same time old and new in the voting theory literature. It is old insofar as the collective choices are often resorted to in resolving conflicts in a peaceful manner. Sometimes, they succeed, but quite often they also fail, especially when majority referenda are arranged, as Emerson points out. It is new in the sense that conflict mitigation or avoidance is seldom elevated to the status of an explicit social choice desideratum. In Emerson's thinking it should be. For what it is worth, I agree. It is this insight together with the rich empirical and comparative material that makes Emerson's book eminently worth studying not only for those unfamiliar with the voting theory, but also for those familiar with it. By introducing the important criterion of conflict avoidance capability, this work paves the way towards a more relevant theory of voting. This theory puts the emphasis on giving the voters reasons to participate and to accept outcomes that do not always coincide with their most favourite options. This emphasis reveals, indeed, the forte of camp (ii) to which Emerson belongs. The reader may disagree—and I gather Emerson would expect and welcome it—on some details of the proposals advocated, but the overarching goal of the enterprise is without any doubt a commendable one. This thought-provoking book deserves to be widely read and discussed. As war has been said to be too important to be left solely for the generals, the institutions of democratic governance are too important to be left solely for the social choice theorists. Nonetheless, as generals in war, the social choice theorists in institutional design are capable of providing essential information about what is within the realm of the possible and what is not.

Hannu Nurmi
Professor Emeritus of Political Science
University of Turku
Turku, Finland

Preface

There is an *idée fixe*, pretty well everywhere: that decisions should be based on the wishes of the majority. Even people like Vladimir Ilyich Lenin and Máo Zédōng (though voting sparingly) spoke of 'the majority' at length. And across the globe, the consequences have been disastrous.

Something is not as it should be. Basically, on questions of complexity, you cannot best identify the collective will of dozens let alone millions by asking a simple, yes-or-no, binary question; logically, it is impossible.

Majority rule is obviously a good thing; but 'binary majority rule' in which decisions are based on majority votes is often hopelessly inaccurate… and therefore sometimes dangerous. There are, however, several ways of identifying a majority opinion, and majority rule need not be binary.

* * * * *

This text is a guidebook for decision-makers all, from members of the local community association to our elected representatives in parliament. It is about decision-making, so there's a lot about the voting procedure, the most important part of decision-making, and hardly anything about electoral systems… until Chap. 7. Granted, many decision-making systems can be used as electoral systems, such as plurality voting which is then called first-past-the-post. Nevertheless, the text tries to distinguish between the two functions.

Having explained in Chap. 1 why win-or-lose majority voting can be at least problematic, there is a full description of a more inclusive and more accurate methodology of decision-making: a win-win preferential points system of voting, and this set of decision-making rules, Chap. 2, should be enough for any chairperson at a local AGM or the speaker in any parliament. What's more, there is an app to help: www.debordavote.org allows all and sundry to use this points system of preferential voting, as and when they please.

For those who would like to understand why preferential voting is so accurate, Chap. 3 is a reasonably detailed guide. To get a more thorough grasp of their duties, the chair and consensors of a decision-making process should go one stage further and read Chap. 4. The next chapter considers the benefits of consensus voting, the biggest of which accrues from the fact that preferential points voting is non-majoritarian, in which case, if the international norm of democratic decision-making were to be based on this more accurate—and therefore more democratic—methodology, the era of binary majority rule could be at an end.

Just to round everything off, Chaps. 6 and 7 look at other voting procedures: the former compares the more common decision-making systems, while the latter—ah, at last—is an overview of electoral systems. Because of PR, these are far more numerous. Now many politicians and others point out that no voting procedure is perfect, and some quote Arrow's impossibility theorem as the proof (Arrow 1963: 85). That might, or might not, be true (Saari 2019: 133–144), but either way, it should not stop anyone from an overall assessment of these various methodologies, so to identify just which systems are often erroneous, which are perhaps a little better, and those which are good or even very good.

Finally, Annex A summarises the role of the consensors; B looks at the way different sets of preferences may be interpreted; and C lists the way consensus coefficients can vary. The book concludes with a glossary of all the terms used and of course an index.

The Text

As a general rule, options are ***A, B, C***... italicised and emboldened; there are just two exceptions, ***X*** and ***Y***. Persons, usually of alternate gender, are *i, j, k*..., and they are italicised. While political parties are ***W, X, Y*** and ***Z***, again italicised and emboldened.

Most books follow the convention that numbers less than ten are spelt out in full, while other larger quantities are in digits. Because there are so many in this text, however, exceptions are frequent, if but for the sake of what the author hopes is clarity. In addition—no pun intended—preferences are ordinal, 1st, 2nd, 3rd … while any other use of these is spelt out: first, second, third, etc. Finally, when talking of the matrix vote (as we do in Chap. 5), the word 'sum' is the number of

Table 1 Sums, Scores and Totals

The cabinet		Ministers of....						Scores
		....	....	....	....	....	....	
Preference	Name							
1st		Sum	Sum	Sum	Sum	Sum	Sum	Score
2nd		Sum	Sum	"	"	"	"	Score
3rd		Sum	"	"	"	"	"	Score
4th		Sum	"	"	"	"	"	Score
5th		"	"	"	"	"	"	Score
6th		"	"	"	"	"	"	Score
Scores		Score	Score	Score	Score	Score	Score	Total

points a candidate may receive for a particular portfolio; a 'score' is the addition of several sums; and a 'total' refers to lots of scores on the guidelines shown in Table 1.

Terminology

That which is often called 'the paradox of voting' is more specifically called 'the paradox of [binary] voting'.

Many people know that minority rule was wrong. On that basis, and in the knowledge that unanimity is at the very least unlikely, they assume that which must be the opposite—majority rule—must be right. As shall be seen in the text, however, while there is only one form of binary voting—the (simple or weighted) yes-or-no majority vote—there are many types of multi-option voting: some single preference, a few non-preferential and others multi-preference. In other words, there are many ways of determining a majority opinion, some more accurate (as we shall see) than others.

It follows that there must be a number of different forms of majority rule. One of them—binary majority rule—is ubiquitous and often iniquitous. But majority rule governance could also be based on a different more accurate voting methodology. Accordingly, this book introduces the term, 'preferential majority rule'.

Acknowledgements

'Right kids, what's for lunch, broccoli?' By a substantial majority, the will of the kids is no broccoli. 'OK, what about turnips?' Ughhh, they scream even more loudly. Nope, that loses as well. The children's collective will is no broccoli and no turnips. Swedes? Another no. So beware: as in the playgroup, so too in politics, asking yes-or-no votes on every single thing could mean you finish up with nothing. I get the impression that most people understand this: friends, colleagues and many acquaintances—everybody, it seems, except countless professionals in the media, most in politics and everyone in the UK Electoral Commission.

Instead, in the world at large, it is often assumed that, if a vote has been held, the outcome is, *ergo*, democratic. As Hannu Nurmi notes in his foreword, however, for any given electorate with a given set of preferences, the outcome may sometimes depend almost entirely on the voting methodology. 'It's not the people who vote that count, it's the people who count the votes', was how one Josef Stalin put it, for even with majority voting, a little cheating may sometimes be necessary.

Secondly, when people talk about voting, they often discuss electoral systems. The latter can and do vary enormously, and apparently, that's OK; nevertheless, it seems, nearly all these systems are also regarded as democratic. As noted already, maybe nothing's perfect, so imperfections are inevitable… and that's OK too, well sort of. In stark contrast lies the virtually non-existent debate about decision-making:[5] it varies hardly at all, and the voting methodology is nearly always the worst: this simplistic (simple or weighted) majority vote.

My own efforts at questioning this obsession with binary voting go back to 1977, with a little letter in the Belfast-based newspaper, the *Irish News*. There was no response. So my thoughts were put into practice, not least with the help of colleagues in the New Ireland Group, NIG, and my especial thanks go to its founder, the late Dr John Robb. Our first 'experiment in consensus' was in 1986, a public meeting of over 200 persons—politicians from all sides and paramilitaries of both, along with many other persons of neither: they used preferential points voting, and sure enough, they found their consensus. 'Only in years to come', John said when it was all over, 'will people come to learn of the significance of this day'.

Prototypes of the voting procedures described in this book were thus put to the test and, in later public meetings, developed further. In 1991, for example, we first used electronic voting. And there have been umpteen demonstrations of consensus voting since, not only in Ireland, North and South, and in Britain, but also elsewhere in Europe, as well as in Africa, America and most recently in Asia.

But back to the early 1980s and, at the first Convention of the Irish Green Party in 1982, I gave a seminar on consensus voting. One year later, I launched the Northern Irish GP at a press conference in Belfast's infamous (and not very 'green') Europa Hotel.[6] As with the NIG, so too with the Greens, some friendships from those days, most especially with Phil Kearney (on whose Co. Wicklow farm these words are penned), are still strong. And he it was who first suggested we set up the de Borda Institute, in which others like Alan Quilley played a major role—as a good Quaker, he had a natural dislike of any divisive voting procedure. Since then, other colleagues have joined the fray, not least two academics, Katy Hayward and Vanessa Liston, while Mark McCann is our faithful, long-term computer expert.

Many in the NI media have attended one or more of our NIG or de Borda conferences, and two equally cross-community multi-party gatherings I organised for the NIGP—an all-party mini-Earth Summit in Belfast at the time of the UN conference in Rio de Janeiro in 1992 and an all-party debate on power-sharing in 1993 in the town of Dungannon. Now one might have expected the press to be interested in voting systems and the potentially peaceful consequences thereof but, for some

[5]Many social choice scientists are also at fault in this regard. Totally mutually exclusive options are sometimes difficult to find, and even the two sides in the Cold War divide—communist or capitalist—shared a common creed based on human greed, a desire to 'conquer' nature to satisfy that greed. In theory, however, when talking about elections, candidates are always, as it were, mutually exclusive… even when their policies are fairly similar; such was the case, for example, with Josef Stalin and Leon Trotsky. So voting theory often revolves around elections and not decision-making.

[6]So that was nearly 40 years ago. And initially, the Greens were all very consensual: we sat in circles, we started in silence, and we used consensus voting. Today, however, while a Borda methodology is still used in some internal party elections, it is seldom deployed in its primary function of decision-making, while the matrix vote was adopted and then just quietly forgotten.

reason, many just wanted to interview the representative(s) from *Sinn Féin*.[7] Academia wasn't much better: when we approached Queen's University for a venue in 1986, we were told such a cross-community conference would be far too dangerous—so we used the Students' Union instead… whereupon, to be fair, some academics crossed the road to see what was going on. In general, however, one can't help getting the impression that professors don't like to debate professional matters with persons like the current author who never even graduated.

There are of course the exceptions, and the most notable were the late Professors Elizabeth Meehan in Belfast and Sir Michael Dummett in Oxford. Amongst those very much alive and still kicking hard, professors all, are (from West to East) Donald Saari and Arend Lijphart, both in California, Don Horowitz in North Carolina, John Barry (Belfast), John Baker (Dublin), Iain McLean (Oxford), Maurice Salles (Caen), Hannu Nurmi (Turku), Sasha Rusetsky (Tbilisi), Fuad Aleskerov (Moscow), Yáng Lóng 杨龙 (Tiānjīn), Sòng Yíngfā 送迎发 (Xúzhōu) and Chāo Yung-Màu 趙永茂 (Taipei). Not quite so well decorated, perhaps, are colleagues in openDemocracy, like Rosemary Belcher; fellows in the Royal Society for the Arts, Manufactures and Commerce such as Matthew Taylor; friends in the Conflict Research Society, Andrew Thompson et al.; and professionals like Michael Emerson (no relation) in Central European Political Studies in Brussels. Yet others with even more modest qualifications include some of my best friends, not least Wes Holmes of the NIG, who still gives me magnificent, often liquid support.

Rather fewer journalists have shown any interest in voting systems, so life has sometimes been a little frustrating. In 1990, for example, out of total exasperation, I met with the controller of BBC NI and asked why the subject of consensus could not be covered, at least once. 'We need a hook', he said, 'and once there is a story, we can then debate the topic'. So I learnt some Serbo-Croat (which wasn't too difficult as I already spoke Russian) and went to Bosnia to work as a freelance correspondent, cycling, in winter and in war, from Zagreb via Banja Luka to Belgrade, and back via Zvornik and Sarajevo to Split. BBC NI? Not interested. They don't do books either, not mine anyway. Book launches in the House of Lords with the late Lord Paddy Ashdown? *In Áras an Uachtaráin*, his official residence, with President Michael D Higgins? No, not good enough, boy.

So, going back a little, in 1994, I turned my attention to London, BBC Radio 4, and 25 years later—ah, at last!—it paid off, but mainly because Britain was then going bonkers over its binary Brexit: I did two interviews, with one on its famous *Today* programme. More recently, I travelled overland (of course) with my fold-up bicycle (of course) on two year-long lecture tours, from Belfast to Beijing and beyond; I gave talks on preferential decision-making in universities and the like in 15 different jurisdictions, including Iran, Russia and China. The media at home were interested… but only when I was evacuated from Gansu because of COVID-19. In my work on voting systems? No no.

[7]The best way to get a journalist to attend a function, by the way, especially a public meeting on a Saturday, is to ask them to take the chair. Ha, perfect; you've got 'em for the entire day!

Overall, then, media coverage has been minimal. Billy Graham and Noel Doran of the *Irish News* were fine exceptions; Andy Pollak and Joe Humphreys of the *Irish Times*, two more; and eventually, the BBC's Evan Davies and Justin Webb of Radio 4 actually mentioned names and voting procedures like de Borda and Condorcet. Meanwhile, on the social media network, the long-serving peace activist Rob Fairmichael is a strong supporter. So far, however, that's just about it.

In the light of such discouragement, friends have been vital. Indeed, without them, most of whom agree with my ideas though not always with the supporting mathematical arguments, this book would not have been written. I start with Dervla Murphy, who first launched me on my literary endeavours in 1978—her disdain of politicians and their shenanigans is exemplary. By this time, of course, the NI peace movement was underway, and I still get exhortations and encouragements from Mairead Corrigan Maguire. Overall, however, the NI response has invariably been rather muted.

So as noted, I had to go abroad and campaign there as well, and the list now extends to many lands. Apart from those I have already mentioned, there are umpteen others too, many of whom have been my hosts… and this time we go from first to most recent: they include Leo Joosten (Leiden), an old pal from the 1970s when we took a bunch of kids cycling to Donegal; Angela Mickley (Berlin) who again dates back from those heavy days in Belfast and who has hosted many seminars on consensus politics in her university in Potsdam; along with Phil Kearney, Jeremy Wates (Brussels) was also at the first Irish Green Party convention in 1982; in 1986, it was time for the bicycle again, so off I went to meet another cyclist and then my co-author, Irina Bazileva (Moscow); Nato Kirvalidze was one of half-a-dozen to greet me in Tbilisi in 1990, where I gave a press conference (in Russian—my Georgian is no good) on power-sharing at the invitation of the late Zurab Zhvania MP; and shortly afterwards in the Balkans, I started a partnership with Věra Stojarová (Brno)—we co-edited a book together—and Valery Perry (Sarajevo), who writes her own; in the year 2006, the French Green Party was having an argument, a potential split, so Vicky Selwyn (Normandy) invited me to France to talk to a whole load of French people about a Frenchman they'd never heard of—the good Jean-Charles de Borda; and next came Marcin Gerwin, who asked me to give a presentation or two in Warsaw in 2009. Finally, on my two overland journeys across Eurasia when I was again looked after by nearly all of the above, I also met Albert Franz, who started my grand tour by inviting me to give a TEDX talk in Vienna in 2017; then came Anushka Danoyan and Tatev Karapetyan (Yerevan), Sarafraz Hossein (Tehran), George Cautherley (Hong Kong) and, finally, my latest 2020 additions, Marina Nizar and William Tham (Kuala Lumpur).

To everyone who has made this book possible, to all of the above, thank you; to Hannu Nurmi again, a special word of thanks for his long-term support which now culminates in the foreword; and once more to Rob Fairmichael, who still corrects all my spelling mistakes, and quite a few others besides. A special word of commiseration is due to all those constitutional wallahs who, having read these pages, will have to amend their umpteen rules and regulations in countless preambles and subclauses in numerous articles, contracts and standing orders. Lastly, but crucially, I give my thanks to Johannes Glaeser and colleagues in Heidelberg, my patient publishers in Springer.

Wicklow, Ireland Peter Emerson
May 2020

References

Arrow, K. (1963). *Social Choice and Individual Values* (2nd ed.). New Haven: Yale University Press.

Saari, D. G. (2019). Arrow, and Unexpected Consequences of his Theorem. *Public Choice*, 179(1).

Contents

Abbreviations

AGM	Annual general meeting
AV*	Alternative vote
BC	Borda count
DPRK	Democratic People's Republic of [North] Korea
EC/U	European Commission/Union
EEC	European Economic Area
FPTP	First-past-the-post
IRV*	Instant run-off voting
MBC	Modified BC
MLA	Member of the legislative assembly (NI)
MMP	Multi-member proportional
MP	Member of Parliament
NI	Northern Ireland
NZ	New Zealand
OSCE	Organization for Security and Co-operation in Europe
PM	Prime minister
PNG	Papua New Guinea
PPV	Preferential points voting
PR	Proportional representation
PV*	Preference voting
QBS	Quota Borda system
SNTV	Single non-transferable vote
STV*	Single transferable vote
TRS	Two-round system
UK	United Kingdom
UN	United Nations

US(A) United States (of America)
WTO World Trade Organization

* Four different names for the same system. When used in decision-making or in elections in single-seat constituencies, it is normally referred to as AV; in multi-member constituencies with PR, the system is called PR-STV. AV is also called IRV in North America; while in Australasia, if it's used as an electoral system, it is called AV; in decision-making, it is referred to as PV, preference voting.

List of Figures

List of Tables

List of Graphs

Chapter 1
The Problem

Abstract There are times when majority voting does not work well. Indeed, occasionally, this supposed methodology of resolving disputes only exacerbates them! Binary voting is ancient, divisive and, at worst, a provocation to violence. Yet its use is ubiquitous. This book suggests a more democratic way, but first, let us consider the theory of decision-making.

1.1 Introduction

Binary voting is used in law, as in 'guilty or innocent?' verdicts; in decision-making in business, with majority shareholdings and so on; in countless associations, trade unions, societies and clubs, when resolutions are debated; and in politics whenever policies are ratified with laws to be enacted. Even in the UN Security Council on matters of huge complexity, the final question is often yes-or-no and for-or-against (and the big boys have a veto).

But binary voting is the basis of that which has caused so many problems in so many places, worldwide: binary majority rule. People believe in majority rule, which is fine. But they then assume that a majority opinion can be found by means of a majority vote, which is not fine at all and, what's more, it's not true. As we shall see in Chap. 2, majority voting is often erroneous, while Chap. 6 will show that there are lots of ways of identifying a majority opinion; for the moment at least, we will refer (a) to 'binary majority rule' which can be not only horribly unfair, but also, in some jurisdictions, dysfunctional if not downright dangerous, and (b) to 'preferential majority rule' which could be so much better. Suffice here to say that binary majority rule was a major cause of the Troubles in Northern Ireland; of the genocide in Rwanda which started with the slogan '*Rubanda Nyamwinshi*' 'we are the majority' (Prunier 1995: 185); of mayhem in the Balkans, where 'all the wars in the former Yugoslavia started with a referendum', (*Oslobodjenje*,[1] 7.2.1999) and of many other horrible tragedies—not least, Soviet bolshevism (para 5.1).

[1] Sarajevo's famous newspaper.

P. Emerson, *Democratic Decision-making*,
SpringerBriefs in Political Science,
https://doi.org/10.1007/978-3-030-52808-9_1

Table 1.1 A party divided

Preferences	Ms i	Mr j	Ms k
1st	***A***	***B***	***C***

Democracy was not meant to be just for a fraction, the bigger 'half', a faction of maybe only 50% + 1; democracy is for (almost) everybody. So let's first have a look at the theory of decision-making; and it must be emphasised, this book is mainly about just that, decision-making. Voting is also used in elections, of course, and sometimes here too the methodology is that of the majority vote; indeed, several forms of voting which are used in decision-making may also be used in elections. But again I emphasise, this book is mainly about decision-making.

1.2 A Scenario

First, then, the theory. Imagine a simple scene: the Pink Party office has a pink front door. Ms *i*, a member of the three-person executive, wants to add a white peace symbol and moves a motion to this effect; Mr *j* proposes an amendment, some green stripes instead; Ms *k* suggests purple spots. So there are (at least) four possibilities:

Option ***A***	-	pink with a white symbol;
Option ***B***	-	pink with green stripes;
Option ***C***	-	pink with purple spots;
Option ***D***	-	the *status quo ante*, plain pink.

The debate ensues: 'We must show our peaceful intent', says Ms *i*; 'our environmental credentials', opts Mr *j*; 'our feminist principles', opines Ms *k*. In summary, all three have different 1st preferences, as shown in Table 1.1, and the task is to resolve these differences in a civilised, democratic manner.

1.3 The Theory of Majority Voting

Maybe the democratic thing to do is to use majority voting. Well, there are two types: the first is based on a simple 'yes-or-no?' question, either on one particular option, as in 'Option ***X***, yes-or-no?' or perhaps there could be a single question for each of a number of options; in this instance, the four of them listed above are ***A***, ***B***, ***C*** and ***D***. The second sort of question offers a choice of two options: 'Option ***X*** or option ***Y***?' So with these four options, there are six possible 'pairings', as they are called: ***A*** or ***B?*** ***A*** or ***C?*** ***A-D?*** ***B-C?*** ***B-D?*** and ***C-D***?

Well, if the debate is to be resolved by majority votes of the former variety, and if all three committee members vote in favour of only their 1st preference, guess what,

Table 1.2 A party very divided

Option	*A*	*B*	*C*	*D*
Majority votes	1:2	1:2	1:2	0:3

Table 1.3 A party equally divided

Preferences	Ms *i*	Mr *j*	Ms *k*
1st	*A*	*B*	*C*
2nd	*B*	*C*	*A*
3rd	*C*	*A*	*B*

as with the kids in the preface, there'll be a majority against every option: every single thing loses, as shown in Table 1.2.

So that's no good. Maybe, therefore, the dispute should be resolved in two votes, in which case, we need to know the three persons' preferences; let us assume they are as in Table 1.3.

Let the first majority vote be a contest between ***A*** and ***B***; well the two women both prefer ***A*** to ***B*** and only the man prefers ***B*** to ***A***—so ***A*** wins. In the second majority vote, the decider, it's a vote for the winner, ***A*** versus ***C***, and both Mr *j* and Ms *k* prefer ***C*** to ***A***, so the collective will is for option ***C***. Fine. By 67%. That's a huge majority.

But hang on a minute. If the first round is between ***B*** and ***C***, which ***B*** wins, then the final will be between ***B*** and ***A***, which is a victory for ***A***. That's fine too, and equally hugely so.

Or, hang on again: with a first round of ***C*** versus ***A***, the second round is ***C*** versus ***B***, and the popular choice will now be ***B***, by (again) a massive 67%. Fine?

In this setting, then, the outcome, the *totally democratic decision* of all three, is either ***A*** or ***B*** or ***C***; it all depends on the order of voting. To summarise, then, the two types of majority voting: with '***X***, yes-or-no?' the answer is nothing; and with '***X*** or ***Y***?' it might be anything.

1.3.1 Doing It All by Halves

Maybe a more reliable decision could be ascertained with these 'Option ***X*** or option ***Y***?' questions or pairings, if we took all four possible outcomes into consideration. Let it be assumed the three persons' preferences are as shown in Table 1.4.

And, oh dear, there is still a winner from every pairing, as is now shown in Table 1.5.

Overall, in this instance, option ***A*** is more popular than ***B***, which is written as

$$\boldsymbol{A} > \boldsymbol{B}.$$

Table 1.4 A party even more divided

Preferences	Ms *i*	Mr *j*	Ms *k*
1st	***A***	***B***	***C***
2nd	***B***	***C***	***D***
3rd	***C***	***D***	***A***
4th	***D***	***A***	***B***

Table 1.5 The pairings

Pairings	***A:B***	***A:C***	***A:D***	***B:C***	***B:D***	***C:D***
Majority votes	2:1	1:2	1:2	2:1	2:1	3:0

and in like manner,

$$\boldsymbol{B} > \boldsymbol{C} \text{ and } \boldsymbol{C} > \boldsymbol{D} \text{ and } \boldsymbol{D} > \boldsymbol{A}.$$

So in all, we can say

$$\boldsymbol{A} > \boldsymbol{B} > \boldsymbol{C} > \boldsymbol{D} > \boldsymbol{A}\ldots\ldots\ldots$$

and it goes on and on for ever. This 'cycle' is also called 'the paradox of [binary] voting': no matter what the outcome, there's always a majority which prefers something else.

1.3.2 The Conclusion on Majority Voting

In effect, then, majority voting might work if and when there are only two options (which on contentious topics in politics, as we shall see, should be seldom if at all). But it doesn't work well if there are more than two options. Indeed, with 'Option ***X***, yes-or-no?' questions, if there is no majority *for* any single option, there will be a majority *against* every damned option—a scenario first noted by Pliny the Younger in CE 105; and if we use 'Option ***X*** or option ***Y***?' questions, we might find that there's a binary paradox, as first noted by Le Marquis de Condorcet in 1785.[2]

In a modern pluralist democracy, however, whenever the political subject under debate is complex and/or contentious, there should be, as it were by definition, more than two options 'on the table'. And not only 'on the table' but also on the ballot paper! I suppose there is one question which is definitely dichotomous: 'Which side

[2]One of the lessons from the Weimar Republic is that, rather than posing an 'Option ***X***, yes-or-no?' ballot, it is wiser to ask an 'Option ***X*** or option ***Y***?' question. Hence, Germany's constructive votes of no confidence: if you want to replace government ***A***, you must first propose an alternative, government ***B***.

of the road shall we drive on?'. Well, only one country—Sweden, in 1955—has ever held a referendum on this thorny question and, believe it or not, the number of options on the ballot paper was actually *three*: 'left', 'right' and 'blank'. This meant that those committed democrats who on this particular question were actually indifferent, could nevertheless participate in the democratic process, vote 'blank' and thus, as it were, go with the (traffic) flow.

The conclusion is stark: in a pluralist democracy, whenever a serious decision is to be taken in a vote, there should invariably be more than two options on the ballot paper. As mentioned earlier, in a court of law, questions might indeed be binary: guilty or not guilty? But in (business, civic society and) politics, and especially on contentious matters, no. And even if there are only two options in the debate, there may well be (as in Sweden) more than two ways of voting.

By all means take a majority vote on something if the subject is not controversial: 'Shall we now break for coffee, folks? A show of hands please?' But if the topic is at all serious and if there is no consensus for a majority vote, resort should never be made to such an exclusive, divisive and win-or-lose methodology.

1.3.3 The One-Party, One-Option, One-Candidate State

Now many people would dismiss any election which was based on a single nominee—'Candidate ***X***, yes-or-no?' That's the sort of nonsense stuff they have in North Korea (where, to make matters worse, it's more a case of 'Candidate ***X***, yes-or-yes?'). The true democrat would surely insist that elections should offer a range of contestants. Anything which boils down to a 'Candidate ***X***, yes-or-no?' sort of election—like the 'Putin, yes-or-no?' contests in Russia—is pretty meaningless. And anything like a 'Candidate ***X*** or candidate ***Y***?' dichotomy—the sort of 'Trump or Clinton?' two-horse race, as there was in the 2016 US presidential contest—is not much better (and if we weren't talking about the United States, we might even say two donkeys).

In like manner, binary decision-making is just not good enough. The 'Option ***X***, yes-or-no?' referendum—as was used in Britain's 2016 Brexit poll (para 6.2)—was a Pyongyang type of nonsense: a government should never ask a single-option question in a multi-option debate, not if it is then going to pretend that the outcome of such a dichotomy is the collective will. An 'Option ***X*** or option ***Y***?' dichotomy, as in the UK's 2011 referendum on the electoral system was only a slight improvement, for this too was a multi-option debate[3]: for those who wanted PR, proportional representation, that ballot was like asking a vegetarian, 'Beef or lamb?'. As noted earlier, if and when a topic is contentious, decision-making in parliamentary votes and/or in referendums

[3] As we shall see in Chap. 7, there are over 300 electoral systems to choose from, yet David Cameron decided to restrict the choice to just two: the people could choose either his 1st preference or his 2nd.

should invariably be based on a range of options, usually [a short list of] about five of them.

1.4 Majority Voting in Practice

As seen from all of the above, majority voting definitely has its limitations. But yes, it is used pretty well everywhere, even when the debates are indeed multi-optional. Accordingly, because this methodology can be so capricious, and because so much depends upon the order of voting, those who believe in binary voting laid down a number of rules and procedures—what is the minimum quorum; how and when a motion may be proposed and seconded, and then moved; how and in what order to take amendments, additions and even corrigendums, and so it goes on. These rules, however, some at least 2000 years old, cover every detail—except a critique of binary ballots!—but they are not quite as good as the authors of old and today's constitutional lawyers intended.

Let us return to the Pink Party executive committee and its debate over the front door; and let it be assumed that the three members—Ms *i*, Mr *j* and Ms *k*—have the preferences shown above in Table 1.4 and here repeated as Table 1.6.

So, to recap, option ***A*** is the motion, as moved by Ms *i*; option ***B*** will be the motion if the original is amended as Mr *j* has proposed; if Ms *k*'s suggestion is adopted instead, it will become option ***C***; and ***D*** is the status quo ante.

According to the rules, then, the first thing to do is to choose the more preferred amendment: ***B*** or ***C***. So that's the first debate and vote, and both Ms *i* and Mr *j* prefer ***B*** to ***C*** while only Ms *k* prefers ***C*** to ***B***, so by 2:1 it's ***B***. 67% again. The next vote is on whether to amend the motion or leave it as it is: ***A*** versus ***B***, and both women prefer ***A*** to ***B***, so the substantive is now the motion un-amended, option ***A***. The final vote is therefore ***A*** versus ***D***, and both Mr *j* and Ms *k* prefer ***D*** to ***A***, so our second *totally democratic* decision as shown in Fig. 1.1 is option ***D***, and it wins, yet again, by a massive 67%—so who could argue with that? The door is to remain a plain pink.

But wait a moment: all three of them, Ms *i*, Mr *j* and Ms *k*, prefer ***C*** to ***D***. In this instance (and in many another), majority voting is not just inaccurate, it's wrong!

It's a bit like taking the temperature of a coronavirus patient; needless to say, we use thermometers which are calibrated into lots of degrees and not just into two

Table 1.6 A party even more divided

Preferences	Ms *i*	Mr *j*	Ms *k*
1st	***A***	***B***	***C***
2nd	***B***	***C***	***D***
3rd	***C***	***D***	***A***
4th	***D***	***A***	***B***

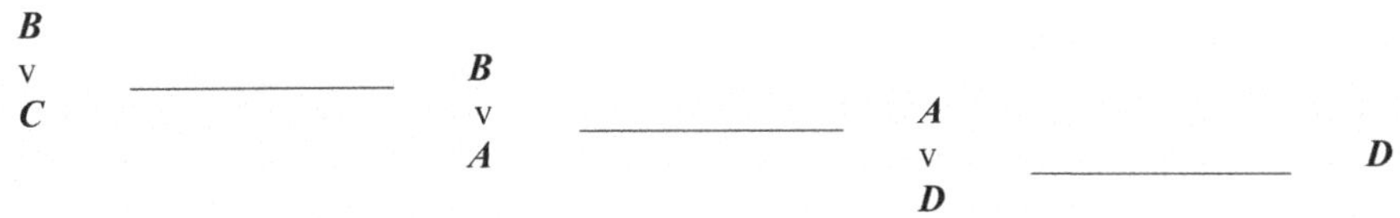

Fig. 1.1 The binary debate

extremes, a binary 'hot' or 'cold'. So too in decision-making, the collective will in many debates will not be either 'black' or 'white' but rather somewhere in the 'grey'. By using binary voting, however, the answer is often 'black' or 'white', and when the true answer should be 'grey', this answer is, as above, wrong!

1.5 Conclusion

So there are indeed those instances when majority voting is imprecise if not indeed hopelessly incorrect. Sometimes, and especially when the problem itself is not binary, a binary procedure just does not work well or, in the worst case scenarios, it doesn't work at all.

1.5.1 'Option X, Yes-or-No?'

Consider the logic. To identify the collective will on any one subject, we first have to identify all the individual wills... but we can't do that if some people are saying not what they want, but only what they don't want, i.e. if they're voting only 'no'.

Furthermore, as it were by definition, the 'will of the people' or the will of parliament or whatever cannot be identified in a binary vote of the 'Option *X*, yes-or-no?' variety, because that option *X* has to be identified earlier if it is to be already on the ballot paper.[4]

Politicians of course like to use majority voting, especially of the 'Option *X*, yes-or-no?' variety. After all, when they choose the question, they control the debate if not indeed the outcome, and in many instances the answer is the question. No wonder majority voting has been the decision-making methodology of choice on those rare occasions when certain dictators have actually preferred to be ostensibly democratic, the likes of, amongst others, Napoléon, Lenin, Mussolini, Hitler, Duvalier, Pinochet, Khomeini, Mugabe and Saddam Hussein (Emerson 2012: 143–50).

---

[4]Admittedly, in theory, it could be done in a small committee, as in the UN Security Council. Those drafting the motion talk with all 15 members, and thus aim for a consensus. So, on the scale writ small, majority voting could perhaps work. In a parliament of hundreds, however, or in a society of millions, it couldn't... and it doesn't (para 5.1, fn 1).

1.5.2 *'Option X or Option Y?'*

At the very least, therefore, the question should be a pairing, and this could work, perhaps, if and only if the entire debate were to consist of only two options. As noted earlier, however, in politics, even on such simple topics as choosing the side of the road to drive on, this should rarely if ever be the case.

Accordingly, from Ireland to North Korea,[5] in constitutions and standing orders and so on, all those words and clauses and sections and paragraphs about simple and/or weighted majorities—volumes and volumes of the stuff—may all be little more than just so much baloney. What follows in Chap. 2 is a guideline for a more rational form of decision-making.

References

Emerson, P. (2012). *Defining democracy*. Heidelberg: Springer.

Irish Government. (1937). *Bunreacht na hÉireann*. Constitution of Ireland. Dublin: Government Publications. Articles 6.1 and 47.2.

Juche. (2017). *The socialist constitution of the Democratic People's Republic of Korea*. Pyongyang: Foreign Languages Publishing House. Article 97.

Prunier, G. (1995). *The Rwanda crisis*. London: C. Hurst and Co.

[5]Article 15, 11-1 of Ireland's *Bunreacht na h'Eireann*, (the Irish Constitution) and North Korea's constitution.

Chapter 2
Decision-Making

Abstract In many binary ballots, the question becomes the answer; and those who draft the question thus control the decision-making process in its entirety. In consensus voting, those who make the final decision—the people in a referendum or the members of the relevant elected chamber in any 'parliamentary' vote—shall participate in the entire decision-making process, in formulating the several options which comprise the ballot paper, as well as in the vote which concludes the process. So, on contentious topics, the debate may well be multi-optional, while the vote itself should be not only multi-optional but, in a truer democracy, preferential.

2.1 Introduction

The basic principle of democratic decision-making is that those concerned should be able to participate, not only in the vote which finalises that decision, but also in formulating the ballot on which that vote is to be conducted. In detail, then:

- those who shall make the decision (and/or their representatives—chosen in an election as for a parliament, or selected in an e-sortition for a citizens' assembly, the latter either in situ or online) shall be able to propose an option;
- all relevant options which comply with a given norm (like the UN Charter on Human Rights) shall be allowed 'on the table' to be summarised, perhaps, on a computer screen and maybe enunciated on a dedicated website;
- in the absence of a verbal consensus, a team of consensors—more about these persons in a moment—shall draw up a [short] list of options;
- eligible participants shall then cast their preferences;
  and finally,
- the consensors shall display the voters' profile and adjudicate on the outcome.

Accordingly, in describing the process of decision-making, this chapter is divided into five sections: starting with para 2.2, we have the options, the consensors, the debate, the vote and then the analysis. But first, a word on how the decision-making process starts.

P. Emerson, *Democratic Decision-making*,
SpringerBriefs in Political Science,
https://doi.org/10.1007/978-3-030-52808-9_2

2.1.1 *The Problem and the Personnel*

If and when a problem arises, in parliament, in a petition or wherever, it must be decided, firstly, in which forum—in the elected chamber, a special commission[1] or a citizens' assembly—is the subject to be debated; secondly, in what manner—in person and/or on the web; and thirdly, how the matter is to be resolved, by a vote in parliament or in a referendum, or whatever.

For the debate to proceed, the following persons will be required:

- a chairperson or Mr/Ms speaker, to oversee the entire process;
- a team of consensors;
- a timekeeper;

and all concerned must know, who shall be eligible to participate in the debate and who may be entitled to vote.

2.1.2 *The Theory*

If there are *x* participants (or *x* Parties) in the debate, there may well be up to *x* different proposals 'on the table', and each option (see below) shall be a complete package—a complete, stand-alone policy option for the problem in question.

As the debate proceeds, with time allocated to each proposal, the total number of proposals, *x*, may be whittled down to a more manageable quantity and if (as is likely in any parliamentary setting whenever the question is contentious) a verbal consensus proves to be illusory, a preferential vote may be held to see which of these options best represent the collective will—if at all.

If one option gains a sufficiently high level of support (again, see below), this option may be deemed to be the final decision. If however all of the options enjoy about the same level of support, or if in other words the outcome of the vote is, or is close to, a dead heat, then maybe there is no consensus and therefore no decision shall be taken[2]; instead, the debate shall be resumed, or whatever, as decided by the chair.

---

[1]In 1992, for example, New Zealand set up an independent commission to chair a debate on the NZ electoral system; it reduced what was definitely a multi-option question to a five-option referendum. The people then voted, to reduce this still further to a single-option decision. In stark contrast, in 2016, the UK held a binary referendum on Brexit (para 6.2), and only *after* the poll was there then a debate—or rather a bloody great argument—about the various options.

[2]In consensus politics, policies should never be adopted or rejected by a margin of only one vote: see https://www.deborda.org/won-by-one/

2.2 The Options

Every option shall be, yes, a complete package. In other words, there shall be no formal amendments as such (and no binary votes on them either).[3] Instead, if somebody or some party wishes something to be a little or a lot different from the original motion, they should rewrite the entire proposal, highlighting those small or large section(s) which they want to be different. They may even want something which is completely different, and that too is acceptable… as long as their alternative proposal is a cohesive whole policy.

Any one participant or party may propose only one option.

Every proposed option shall be accepted—as is often said in peace negotiations, everything shall be 'on the table'—as long as, in the opinion of the consensors, the said proposal complies with some previously agreed norm like the UN Charter on Human Rights.

2.3 The Consensors

The consensors shall be a team of at least three persons, impartial and non-voting. In many a setting, as might happen in a citizens' assembly, they may be three or more experts on the matter(s) under discussion. They may be selected beforehand or elected (ideally, in a preferential and proportional methodology—see Chap. 7) by the participants. In a parliament, a more permanent team could be elected from members of the judiciary.

Their job can be quite difficult.[4] Initially, having accepted both the substance and the format of the original motion, they may offer their advice on this format to those who may wish to propose an alternative option. As and when the various options are submitted, the consensors may draw up a list of these options in the knowledge that, in the absence of any verbal consensus at the end of the debate, it may be necessary for them to edit the list, not least to ensure that it is 'balanced'—of which there is more in para 4.2.

If need be, the full list of options can be detailed on a dedicated web page, with as mentioned any differences between the original motion and any later proposals highlighted as necessary. At the same time, a summary can be shown to the participants in any in situ setting on a computer screen. The consensors' duties cover a number of other items as well, as we shall see, and a full list of all their responsibilities is detailed in Annex A.

---

[3] There can never be, therefore, a wrecking amendment.

[4] But better that, of course, than relying on a simplistic binary vote, the consequences of which might be complex if not indeed tragic—as for example in the referendums of the 1990s in the Balkans, let alone the binary ballots of the dictators we mentioned (para 1.5.1).

2.4 The Debate

In the debate itself, participants in situ or online shall be limited in their contributions, either in time by a set of 'traffic lights'[5] or by a fixed maximum number of words, respectively. These limitations will have been previously agreed to by the consensors: so many minutes or words for anyone moving a policy proposal; with smaller quantities for any further contributions, to query or criticise or seek clarifications or suggest amendments[6] or whatever. A further limitation will apply to the number of times any one participant or party can make an intervention, and the total number and duration of the various individuals' contributions may be recorded on a further display.

If at any time the consensors feel that two options are very similar and could therefore be composited, they may suggest this and, if the two movers agree, facilitate such. For the sake of balance in the list of options, they might also suggest that another option or two should be proposed. Or if, as the debate proceeds, it appears that a particular option is losing support and if its original mover agrees, they might indicate that it could be withdrawn. At all times, however, the consensors should ensure that the total list of options is balanced.

So the number of options under discussion may vary. If at the end of the day that number becomes a singleton, the latter may be regarded as a verbal consensus, and no vote shall be required. If, however, no such verbal agreement appears to be likely, the chair may call for a vote. In which case, the consensors will first draw up a balanced list of about four—six options.[7] If all concerned agree that their original motion has been included either verbatim or as adjusted or in composite, or at the very least debated, this list can then become the ballot.

2.5 The Vote

In consensus voting, nobody votes *against* any other body or any other thing. Nobody votes 'no'. Instead, albeit in their order of preference, voters vote only *in favour* of (one, some or at best) all the various options.

The consensors have already decided that every option listed is a valid aspiration. And every person eligible to vote is now, as it were, asked to cast their preferences

[5]A set of lights visible to all: if 'green', the contributor may (continue to) speak; if 'orange', one minute remains; and if 'red', time is up!

[6]There can still be amendments, of course, but these will not be formally moved and voted on as in any binary debate, the sort of procedures we critiqued in Chap. 1. Maybe 'make suggestions' would be a better term.

[7]The number should always be more than 2. If the number of options is 3, the option as it were in the middle might be seen to be 'the compromise' and might therefore be a more likely outcome. So 4 or 5 may be a good minimum and, if the subject is complex, 6 may be regarded as the maximum.

for all the options listed.[8] Indeed, the way the vote is counted—see below—actually encourages the voters to be inclusive in this way. Accordingly, by casting a full slate of preferences, the voters may (a) recognise the validity of every option listed, each of which, of course, is the aspiration of a neighbour and (b) imply that if the consensus of all concerned is actually in favour of their lowest preference, then they will nevertheless accept this outcome.

Now in a binary vote, the choice is 'this' or 'that' and, as often as not, that's that. In consensus voting, the choice is much greater: in a three-option ballot on options ***A-B-C***, there are actually six different ways of submitting a full ballot:

A-B-C, ***A-C-B***, ***B-A-C***, ***B-C-A***, ***C-A-B*** and ***C-B-A***.

With (two, three), four, five and six options, the choice is of course even greater at (2, 6), 24, 120 and 720 different combinations of options, each expressing a slightly different opinion, or maybe just a nuance.

Needless to say, there is also an accurate way in which the final collective will may be analysed (and there's more on this in para 3.7).

2.5.1 The Mathematics of the Vote

In an n-option ballot where the voters are asked to cast up to n preferences, any one voter may choose to cast m preferences, where obviously $n \geq m \geq 1$. In the count, points are awarded to (1st, 2nd … last) preferences cast according to the rule (m, m-1 … 1).

So,

- he who casts only one preference gives his favourite just 1 point,

  {and nothing to those other options on which he has said nothing}
- she who casts two preferences gives her favourite 2 points

  {and her 2nd choice 1 point};
- and those who cast all n preferences give their favourite n points,

  {their 2nd choice (n-1) points, their 3rd preference (n-2) points, etc.}.

The winning option is the option with the most points. So, as stated, the voter is thus encouraged to cast all his preferences, so to give his favourite the maximum number of points. What's more, the protagonist is incentivised, firstly, to ask her supporters not only to give her option their 1st preferences but to do so in full ballots, and secondly, to campaign amongst her (erstwhile majoritarian) opponents so that they will give her option (not a bottom preference but) a 3rd, say, or even a

[8]If the number of options is n, and if $n \leq 10$, the voters may be asked to cast all n preferences. If $n > 10$, voters may be asked to cast a maximum of, say, 6 preferences.

2nd preference. Thus, the political atmosphere changes, and campaigning becomes altogether more positive; consensus voting is far less adversarial than any binary balloting.[9]

At best—that is, if everyone does cast a full list of *n* preferences—the option with the highest number of points is also the option with the highest average preference. And an average, of course, involves every voter, not just a majority of them. This preferential points procedure of voting—the technical term is the Modified Borda Count, MBC—is inclusive… and non-majoritarian; more on all this in Chap. 6.

The MBC, which caters for partial voting—the term used to describe a ballot in which the voter has cast fewer than *n* preferences, para 4.5.1—should not be (but often is) confused with a Borda count, BC. {The BC uses a different rule—either (n, n-1 … 1) or (n-1, n-2 … 0). The latter formula cannot cater for partial voting and, in a polarised debate, it could tempt the intransigent voter to cast just a 1st preference for his favourite option, so to get the full (n) or (n-1) points, without giving anything at all to any of the other options… in which case, the BC can morph into something little better than a plurality vote.} As we shall see, the MBC (despite its adjective, M) was the original methodology first advocated by Jean-Charles de Borda (Saari 2008: 197); the BC is a distortion of his guidelines, even though it came to be used in his lifetime.

2.5.2 The Consensus Coefficient

The level of support for any one option is measured in what is called a consensus coefficient, CC.

Let the number of voters	=	v
Let the number of options	=	n

{In a full ballot, a 1st preference gets *n* points, a 2nd preference gets (n-1) points, and so on, until the last preference gets just 1 point.}

The maximum score	=	$v.n$
The minimum score	=	$1.n$

The consensus coefficient of any one option is defined as that option's MBC score divided by the maximum score, $v.n$. So the CC of option ***A***,

$$CC_A = \frac{MBC_A}{v.n}$$

[9]As will be mentioned in Chap. 7, preferential voting, as in Australian elections, can encourage inter-party co-operation. Such a positive benefit—and more!—can also be the product of preferential points decision-making, as we shall see.

To take a hypothetical example, if option ***D***, say, gets the maximum possible score—everyone's 1st preference, which is *v.n*—then ***D*** will have a CC_D of *v.n* divided by $v.n = 1.00$. If another option, ***B***, gets everybody's last preference, it will get a CC_B of 1.*n* divided by $v.n = 1/v$. And if option ***A*** gets the absolute minimum of zero, of no preferences at all from any voter, then CC_A will be 0.00. So a CC may vary from 1.00 (which is good) to 0.00 (which is not at all good)—but these are hypothetical figures. Option ***A*** would probably not be on the ballot paper if someone(s) had not proposed it, in which case, no doubt, it would get their 1st or at least one or other of their subsequent preferences.

In real life, votes will be held if and when there is no verbal consensus; if and when there is still disagreement as to what is best. The various options on the ballot will only be there if indeed they have been proposed. So in practice, nothing will get a CC of 1.00 (the 1st preferences of everybody) and nothing will ever get 0.00. In really contentious arguments, the answer should never be 'black' or 'white'—democracy should not be 'win' or 'lose'—the outcome should be 'grey', a compromise, win–win.

2.5.3 A Consequence of the Vote

At best, the outcome of such a preferential vote—'the will of the people' or the will of parliament (and if the electoral system is an accurate one, the two collective wills should be similar)—will be the average or collective will of all concerned. It will not be the *more* preferred choice (based on a dichotomy) of a majority, but the *most* preferred choice of everyone who votes. If this more accurate methodology were to be the international democratic norm, therefore, there would be no (further) justification for binary majority rule.[10] Instead, governance could be based on a more inclusive form, as for example on an all-party, power-sharing, government of national unity, GNU, as we shall see in Chap. 5.

2.5.4 The Analysis

If the final outcome has received a CC greater than a predetermined threshold, the consensors may declare this to be the outcome. If there is no consensus, then no decision should be taken. Instead, the outcome may be regarded as a straw poll, which might indicate a cluster of options which deserve more detailed scrutiny, and maybe a few options which have minimal support and which, therefore, warrant no further study.

---

[10] In binary majority rule, if one party wins a majority of seats in parliament, it can then form the government. And it can pass whichever laws it wants. So how does it choose its policies? Oh, by majority vote of course, that's democracy. But 51% of 51% is only 26%; a majority of a majority is often only a minority. So it's not 'the party' which rules, it's the such-and-such wing of that party. And how does that wing choose its policies? Oh dear: binary majority rule does not even exist!

The essence of consensus voting is compromise. Firstly, as mentioned above, maybe, the protagonists have compromised a little, in drafting their proposals. Secondly, the consensors might have asked two or more participants to compromise and combine their options into a composite. Thirdly, in the vote, everyone is incentivised to state their 2nd and subsequent preferences, i.e. their compromise option(s). And fourthly, in the analysis, if two adjacent options—see para 3.5 for a description of this term 'adjacent'—are most popular and if the formation of a further composite is possible, the consensors may well decide to do exactly that.

2.6 Conclusion

In all, therefore, consensus voting is a methodology by which can be identified the best collective compromise.

Reference

Saari, D. (2008). *Disposing dictators, demystifying voting paradoxes*. Cambridge: Cambridge University Press.

Chapter 3
The A-B-C-D of Voting

Abstract The mathematics of any voting procedure is key and, in consensus voting, these rules of the count help to ensure that the outcome is indeed accurate and fair. Firstly, voters are enabled to cast as many preferences as they wish; secondly, the mathematics encourages everybody to complete a full list of preferences; and thirdly, all preferences cast by all voters are taken into account. Combine these mathematical factors with the fact that all participants or their representatives are able to formulate the options, and the result is an inclusive and accurate methodology. In fact, the consequences of this more sophisticated procedure are several, but this chapter looks only at the numerical logic.

3.1 Introduction

Many people don't like mathematics very much (unless it's all connected with sport). Yet the mathematical consequences of treating policy proposals like different teams, which compete either in a knock-out competition or maybe in a league, are several. Let's have a look.

In any event where there are lots of teams, there are indeed several ways that the competition can be organised. Should the winner be the team which wins the most matches, or the one which loses the least, or the one which has the best goal difference, or whatever. Likewise, in voting, there are numerous ways of doing things. As we shall see in Chap. 6, apart from majority voting, there's plurality voting—which option gets the most 1st preferences; the two-round system TRS—a plurality vote which may be followed by a second-round majority vote; the alternative vote AV, a series of plurality votes based on a knock-out; the Borda count BC, a points system; a system based on pairings called the Condorcet rule; a few variations on these themes and a few others besides.

P. Emerson, *Democratic Decision-making*,
SpringerBriefs in Political Science,
https://doi.org/10.1007/978-3-030-52808-9_3

Table 3.1 A party even more divided

Preferences	Ms *i*	Mr *j*	Ms *k*
1st	***A***	***B***	***C***
2nd	***B***	***C***	***D***
3rd	***C***	***D***	***A***
4th	***D***	***A***	***B***

Table 3.2 A party very divided

Option	***A***	***B***	***C***	***D***
Majority votes	1:2	1:2	1:2	0:3

3.2 A Scenario

Imagine, then, there are four teams called ***A***, ***B***, ***C*** and ***D***, and we want to find the best. Or perhaps we just return to the dilemma of the Pink Party, Table 1.4 (and 1.6) is here repeated as Table 3.1, and we want to find the best policy. OK, let's see what happens if different voting procedures are used.

Let us first go back to majority voting, because this too is often used, even when there are three or more options 'on the table'. What happens is that some guy comes along—often a supposed democrat and sometimes a blatant dictator—and he, it's usually a he, decides which option will compete, full stop. So, let us consider team ***A***. To ask a question in an 'Option ***X*** yes-or-no?' format is like asking ***A*** to compete against the rest. Everybody's on the field; 11 ***A*** players in their colour, against 33 others on the other side; the whistle blows, and guess what, ***A*** loses. If it were ***B***'s fate, and if ***B*** had to face the combined forces of three opponents, ***A***, ***C*** and ***D***, then ***B*** would lose as well.

So if it's a case of 'My policy, yes-or-no?' then, in a pluralist democracy, that policy would probably lose. {So normally, of course, be the ruler Napoléon Bonaparte or David Cameron (as in Brexit),[1] he pretends that there is indeed only one option: it's a clear choice, says he. So there is only one option on the ballot. Lots are on (or under) the table, but only one is on the ballot.}

Overall, then, we return to the four options of Table 1.2, here repeated as Table 3.2, and no matter which option is chosen for the gladiatorial '11-v-33' contest, it loses.

[1]In 2016, the British Premier David Cameron decided to have a referendum on the question, 'The UK in the EU, yes or no?'.

Table 3.3 The pairings

Pairings	*A:B*	*A:C*	*A:D*	*B:C*	*B:D*	*C:D*
Majority votes	2:1	1:2	1:2	2:1	2:1	3:0

Table 3.4 The number of pairings

Option	*A*	*B*	*C*	*D*
Pairings	1	2	2	1

So, let's try the other form of majority voting, a pairing, and the politician chooses two teams. So one team plays just one other team, as in an 'Option ***X*** or option ***Y***?' question, and everyone else just watches. In which case, as with Cameron again in 2011, everything still depends upon him… and his choice of ***X*** and ***Y***.[2]

The result with '***X***, yes-or-no?' is always nothing, and now, with '***X*** or ***Y***?' it's anything, and this is shown in Table 3.3—a repeat of Table 1.5. So in either format, majority voting is just no good.

While we're here, we might just look at these pairings and see which team wins the most, as in Table 3.4. And if the winner, the Copeland winner as it's called, is the option which wins the most pairings, the result in this instance is a draw between ***B*** and ***C***.

3.2.1 Another Scenario?

Now in some competitions, it's sometimes very difficult to know which team is the best, especially if many matches end in draws. Indeed, in a voters' profile like that of Table 3.1, neither TRS nor an alternative vote, AV, would work very well, because of an initial tie of all three options—***A***, ***B*** and ***C***—on a score of 1. But even in this simple example, in a BC or in a modified BC, MBC - if every voter casts a full ballot, there's no difference between the two outcomes… which is why folks are sometimes confused, para 2.5.1—it's 4 points for a 1st preference, 3 for a 2nd and so on. So the scores are ***A***-7, ***B***-8, ***C***-9, ***D***-6, and the BC winner would be option ***C***, which is what even a cursory glance at the table would suggest the outcome should be. And in a Condorcet count, as in Table 3.4, it's that ***B/C*** draw.

So there can be huge variations on the outcome of any vote, as shall be seen in more detail in Chap. 6. Let us first, however, take a look at what the results of a multi-option vote *might* mean. In a binary vote, the two options are just assumed to be totally mutually exclusive—it's either Liverpool or it's Manchester City—so, the

[2]In his earlier referendum in 2011, the choice was between his 1st preference and his 2nd; so he was no less dictatorial. He chose just two of hundreds of electoral systems—and there's more on those in Chap. 7.

vote is taken, 50% + , and that's the answer, even if it requires the casting vote of the chair (or a penalty shoot-out).

In multi-option voting, it's all a little different, for in let us say a five-option debate, maybe not every option can be totally mutually exclusive of every other option and maybe there is room for even more compromise. In other words, maybe the best team of all would be a mix of some Liverpool guys with a few from Manchester and maybe even a Chelsea player. To find a champion team of that excellence would be very difficult, but this sort of sophistication in preference voting is actually quite possible: it's called compromise.

3.3 Deciding How to Decide

Majoritarian politics are very much win-or-lose, so maybe not best suited for a democracy. Consensus voting, in contrast, is a little more complicated, but it can and often does lead to a win–win outcome. We are no longer talking about mutually exclusive football teams.

So, if there are five options on the ballot paper, it may be that one option gets a very high score and is obviously the most popular. Or maybe two options are, as it were, 'neck-and-neck', in which case, the consensors—there's yet more on these persons later on—may well choose a composite. Another possibility is that all the options receive about the same level of support, in which case the consensors may feel that there is no consensus at all and that, as was mentioned earlier, no decision shall yet be taken. But first, a little more theory is necessary. We forget sport and enter the field of conciliation and consensus.

3.4 The Single-Peaked Curve

In some debates, various options may be arranged, as it were, in a spectrum: from high to low, for example, from cheap to expensive, or, say, from left wing to right wing. So let us consider a simple example of tax rates for incomes above some huge figure. In any debate on this issue, probably nobody is going to suggest anything less than zero or more than 100%. So almost inevitably, the debate will have its own maximum and minimum, and let us assume the range is from 40 to 60%. In which case, the consensors may well decide, not on a majority vote on, say, '43% yes-or-no?'—the government's choice, ***X***, yes-or-no?—and not on '43 or 56%?'—the government's versus the opposition's? ***X*** or ***Y***?—but on a balanced list of five options: 40, 45, 50, 55 and 60%, ***A-B-C-D-E***, respectively, to represent approximately if not exactly every party's policy option.

In this setting, we assume that everyone casts a full ballot (of which, more soon follows). Now if Ms *i*'s 1st preference is for 60%, she will probably have a 2nd preference of 55%, a 3rd of 50 and so on.

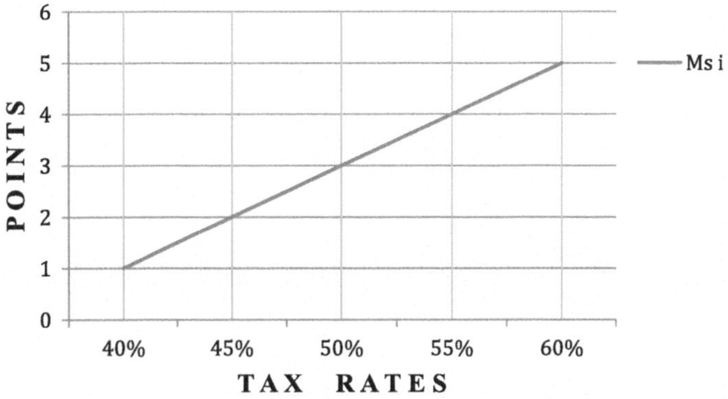

Graph 3.1 A 'single-peaked' curve

60-55-50-45-40
E-D-C-B-A.

Likewise, Mr *j*, whose 1st preference is for 40%, would probably have the following opposite order of preferences:

40-45-50-55-60
A-B-C-D-E.

Ms *k* and M*s l*, on the other hand, might have a different 1st preference: 55%. So Ms *k's* 2nd preference could be 60%, to give her a set of:

55-60-50-45-40
D-C-E-B-A.

or, as with M*s l*, it could be a 2nd preference of 50%, for a set of:

55-50-60-45-40
D-C-E-B-A.

No matter what, however, logically, the set of every voter's preferences should be 'single-peaked', as it is called. Imagine, all the options are laid out on an x-axis, left-to-right, in order; this can be done with tax rates; it cannot be done in a debate on the Pink Party's front door; but it probably could have been done in any debate on Brexit[3] (para 6.2). Then, when most people cast their preferences and these are arranged as in Graph 3.1 for Ms *i*, and Graph 3.2 for all four voters, the effect may

[3] As implied in the current author's press release issued four months before the wretched poll, there could easily have been three or more options ranging from 'remain in the EU' at one end to 'under the World Trade Organisation, WTO' at the other.

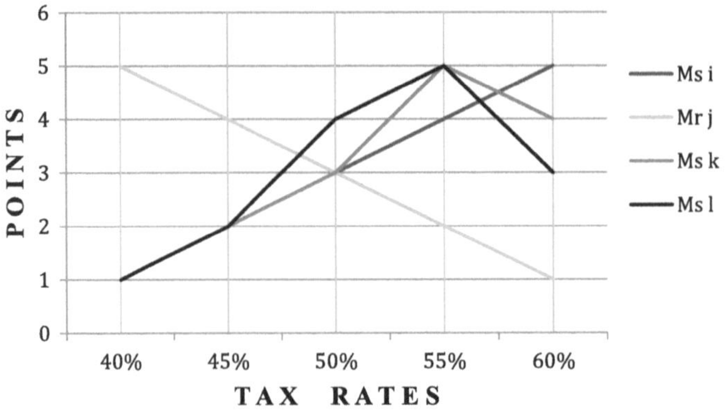

Graph 3.2 Four 'single-peaked' curves

look a bit like a mountain: the 1st preference is at the top, and subsequent preferences slope away on one side and/or the other, hence the term 'single-peaked'.

But back to the tax rates, Ms *i*'s preferences peak at 60%; Mr *j*'s at 40; while Ms *k*'s and Ms *l*'s peak at 55%.

3.4.1 The Collective Will

In any debate, if the options can indeed be ranged in a logical sequence, then every voter's set of preferences should be single-peaked. If they are, then the sum of all these sets of preferences, the voters' collective will, their consensus, will also be single-peaked. Always.

If someone else, however, Mr *m* for example, casts a different set of preferences, something like

45-60-40-55-45
B-D-A-C-E,

the graph of which has two peaks—Graph 3.3—at 45 and 55%, then we can guess that he may be either drunk or drugged.

It could be worse: with preferences of

50-60-40-55-45,
C-E-A-D-B

Mr *n*'s set has three peaks, at 40, 50 and 60. See Graph 3.4. Any MP with such a set of preferences should at least be questioned.

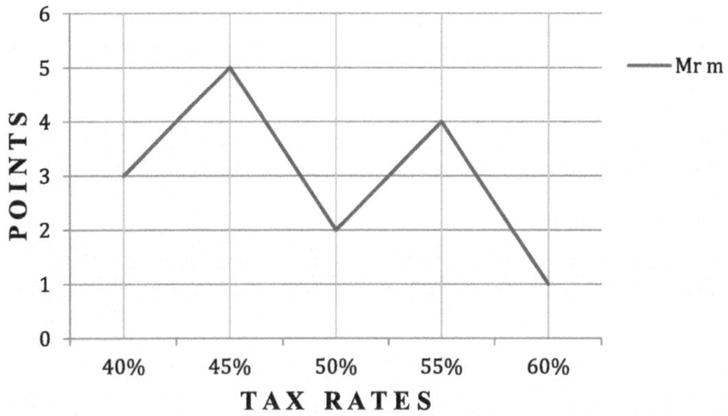

Graph 3.3 An unusual opinion

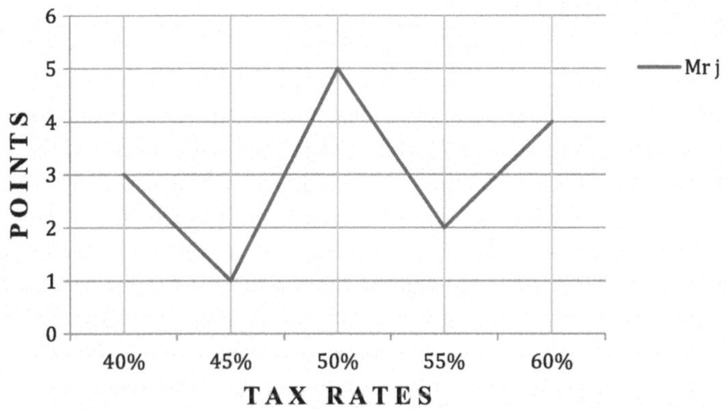

Graph 3.4 A very unsettled set

3.4.2 The Consensus Coefficient

If the options can be sequenced in a logical spectrum, and if everyone does submit a single-peaked set of preferences, the collective will, as I say, will also always be single-peaked. If it isn't, either some of those voting have submitted twin- or triple-peaked curves, and/or some of them have submitted partial votes (see para 3.4.1). For the moment anyway, let's assume that every valid vote is full and single-peaked.

The consensus coefficient, remember, was defined in para 2.5.2. So let us further assume the same three people—Ms *i*, Mr *j* and Ms *k*—cast their preferences on these five options; and that all three voters submit full ballots, each therefore casting all five preferences. Accordingly,

the number of voters		v	=	3		
the number of options		n	=	5		
the number of points/vote	=	5 + 4 + 3 + 2 + 1	=	15		
and the total number of points cast	=	3 x 15	=	45		

So the maximum score of three 1st preferences	=	$v.n$	=	3 x 5	=	15
the minimum score of three 5th preferences	=	$v.1$	=	3 x 1	=	3
and the average score	=					9
(although the absolute minimum	=					0.)

CC_{MAX}	=	15/15	=	1.00
CC_{MIN}	=	3/15	=	0.20
CC_{MEAN}	=	9/15	=	0.60
while				
($CC_{ABS.\ MIN}$	=	0/15	=	0.00)

3.5 Possible Outcomes

Now as in any mountain range, peaks may vary. If the collective will has a single peak which is precipitous at, say 55%, then maybe the consensors will interpret the result to be exactly that, a collective will for 55%. If, however, the mountain is not so steep, and if the two leading options are, say, 55% and 50%—so they are ‘adjacent’, i.e. next to each other on the spectrum of options—the consensors may well decide to compromise and choose a slightly different final tax rate of, say, 54%. (The mathematics, as we shall see, can be quite precise.) As always, in consensus voting, compromise is key: few if any win everything, many if not all win something.

If the most popular option’s level of support is very high, it may be assumed that it has overwhelming support; if it’s only so-so, maybe it’s a consensus; and if it’s only marginally above the mean, the outcome may best be described as the best possible compromise.

3.5.1 Overwhelming Support

In this scenario, opinions are almost unanimous: the 1st preferences are all the same, and so too the 2nd preferences—there’s just a slight variation of viewpoint with regard to their 3rd and 4th preferences, and all is shown as in Tables 3.5 and Table 3.6, while their two single-peaked curves are in Graph 3.5.

Ms *i*’s preferences	55-50-45-60-40	=	***D-C-B-E-A***
Mr *j*’s preferences	55-50-45-60-40	=	***D-C-B-E-A***
Ms *k*’s preferences	55-50-60-45-40	=	***D-C-E-B-A***

So sure enough, as depicted in Graph 3.6, the collective peak is now a very steep pinnacle, centred on 55% but loaded towards the left, so maybe—we shall see—the outcome is 54%.

Table 3.5 The three voters' almost unanimous preferences

Options	1st	2nd	3rd	4th	5th
A					3
B			2	1	
C		3			
D	3				
E			1	2	

Table 3.6 The three voters' almost unanimous points

Options	1st = 5 points	2nd = 4 points	3rd = 3 points	4th = 2 points	5th = 1 point	MBC score	Consensus Coefficient
A					3	3	0.20
B			6	2		8	0.53
C		12				12	0.80
D	15					15	1.00
E			3	4		7	0.47

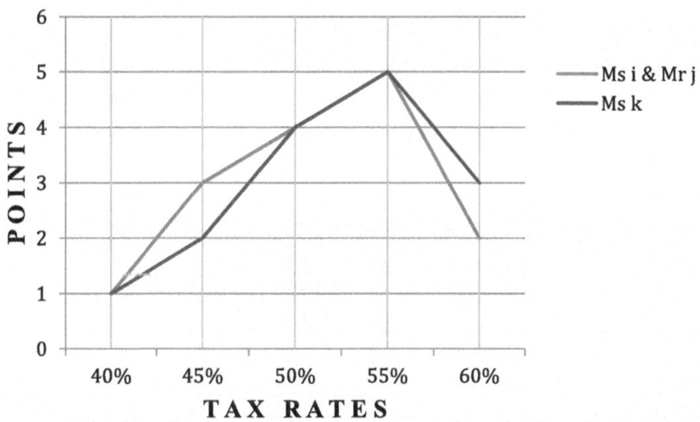

Graph 3.5 The three voters' almost unanimous curves

3.5.2 A Consensus

Consider now another setting: the voters have the following rather different preferences

Ms *i*'s preferences	55-50-45-60-40	=	***D-C-B-E-A***
Mr *j*'s preferences	55-60-50-45-40	=	***D-E-C-B-A***
Ms *k*'s preferences	50-45-55-40-60	=	***C-B-D-A-E***

and their preferences and points, as shown in Tables 3.7 and 3.8, correspond to

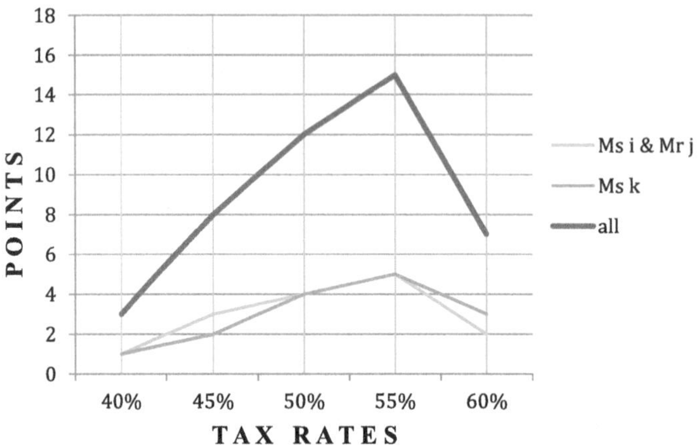

Graph 3.6 The three voters' almost unanimous collective will

Figs. 3.6 and 3.8. Options ***D*** and ***C*** both seem to be pretty popular; support for ***B*** and ***E*** is less, while opposition to ***A*** is still strong.

The same information can be depicted graphically, as shown in Graph 3.7.

There's certainly a fair degree of agreement here, and the resulting collective will, Graph 3.8, is a fairly steep mountain. It peaks at 55% but the 'mountain' is definitely more to the left than to the right, so again, the outcome, to the nearest whole number, is probably 54%.

Table 3.7 The three voters' rather different preferences

Options	The Numbers of Preferences				
	1st	2nd	3rd	4th	5th
A				1	2
B		1	1	1	
C	1	1	1		
D	2		1		
E		1		1	1

Table 3.8 The three voters' rather different points

Options	The Numbers of Points					MBC score	Consensus Coefficient
	1st	2nd	3rd	4th	5th		
A				2	2	4	0.27
B		4	3	2		9	0.60
C	5	4	3			12	0.80
D	10		3			13	0.87
E		4		2	1	7	0.47

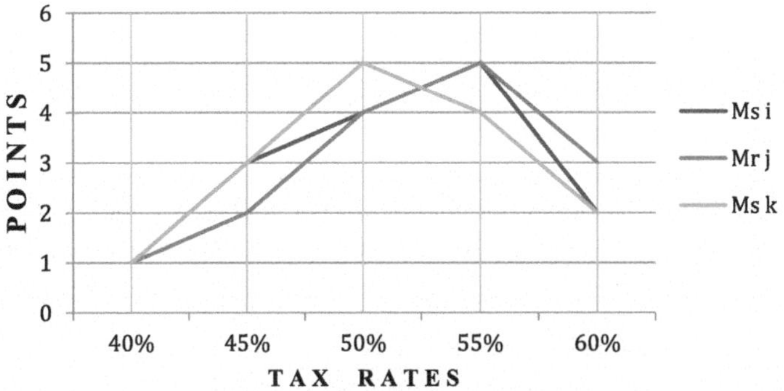

Graph 3.7 The three voters' rather different curves

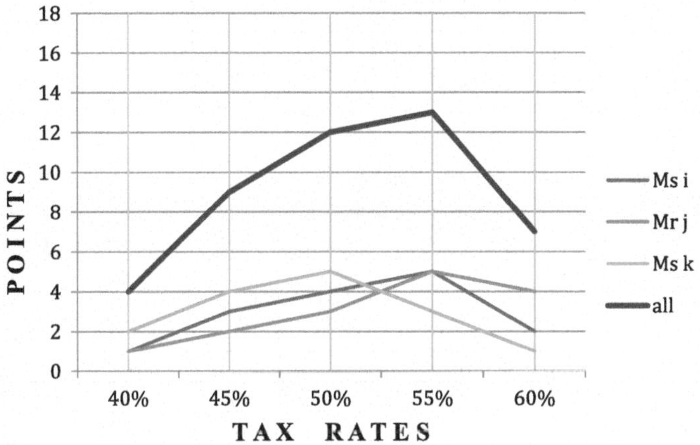

Graph 3.8 The three voters' consensus

3.5.3 Best Possible Compromise

In a 'marginally above the mean' setting, there is not much consensus. Imagine all three now have rather mixed 1st preferences, and the only consensus appears to be a dislike of option ***A***.

Ms *i*'s preferences	55-50-45-60-40	=	***D-C-B-E-A***
Mr *j*'s preferences	45-50-55-40-60	=	***B-C-D-A-E***
Ms *k*'s preferences	60-55-50-45-40	=	***E-D-C-B-A***

So their total preferences are as in Table 3.9, and their total points are in Table 3.10

Sure enough, as in Graph 3.9, all three voters' preferences can again be seen as 'curves' and all are 'single-peaked'.

When these three curves are collated (collected), i.e. when their MBC points are totalled (as in Table 3.10), the result, their collective will, as in Graph 3.10, is a rather flat mountain, but here too the result is a best possible compromise of about 54%.

Table 3.9 The three voters' rather mixed preferences

Options	The Numbers of Preferences				
	1st	2nd	3rd	4th	5th
A				1	2
B	1		1	1	
C		2	1		
D	1	1	1		
E	1			1	1

Table 3.10 The three voters' rather mixed points

Options	The Numbers of Points					MBC scores	Consensus Coefficient
	1st	2nd	3rd	4th	5th		
A				2	2	4	0.27
B	5		3	2		10	0.67
C		8	3			11	0.73
D	5	4	3			12	0.80
E	5			2	1	8	0.53

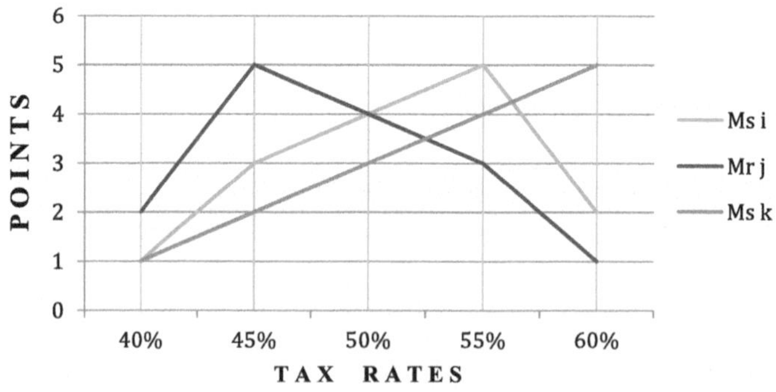

Graph 3.9 The three voters' rather mixed curves

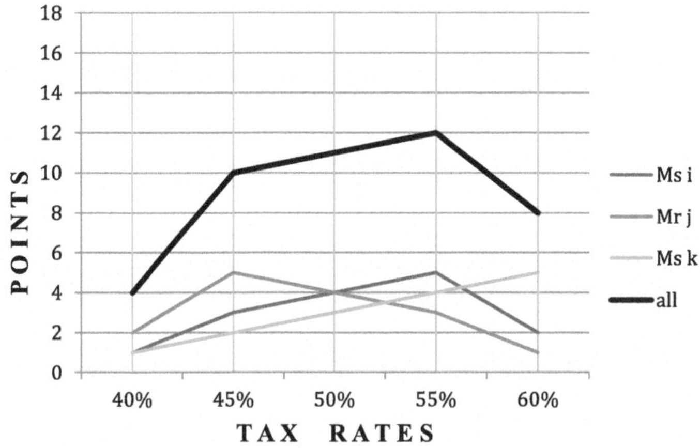

Graph 3.10 The three voters' best compromise

3.5.4 Discord

There will be times, of course, when there is no consensus. Consider the situation when the three voters have the following opinions:

45-40-50-55-60	=	***B-A-C-D-E***
55-60-50-45-40	=	***D-E-C-B-A***
50-45-55-60-40	=	***C-B-D-E-A***

So none of them share the same 1st preferences, and the corresponding preferences and points table are as shown in Table 3.11.

Here, then, as seen in Graph 3.11, the collective peak is more like a plateau. Based on this sort of information, the consensors could well decide that, for a result to become a binding decision, the minimum CC should be 0.75.

The full set of outcomes and their descriptions are shown in Table 3.12.

Table 3.11 The three voters' discord

Options	1st= 5 points	2nd= 4 points	3rd= 3 points	4th= 2 points	5th= 1 point	MBC score	Consensus Coefficient
A		1=4			2=2	6	0.40
B	1=5	1=4		1=2		11	0.73
C	1=5		2=6			11	0.73
D	1=5		1=3	1=2		10	0.67
E		1=4		1=2	1=1	7	0.47

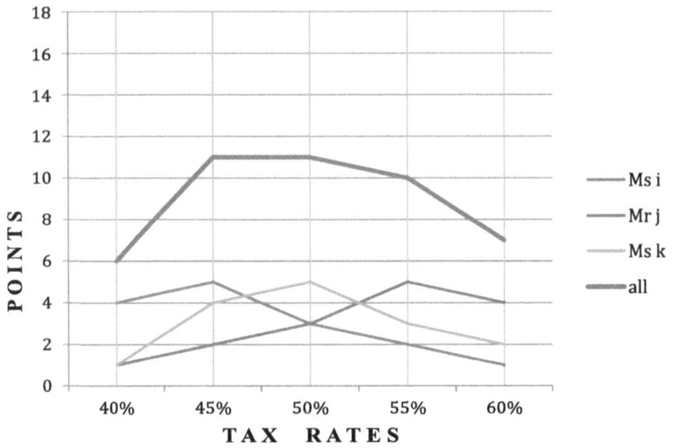

Graph 3.11 The three voters' discord

Table 3.12 Outcomes of a five-option ballot

The Outcome	Consensus Coefficients	
	≥	≤
No consensus	-	0.75
Best possible compromise	0.75	0.80
Consensus	0.80	0.90
Overwhelming support	0.90	1.00

3.6 Analysing the Outcome

As shown in Tables and Figs. 3.6, 3.8 and 3.10, outcomes may vary; sometimes, the winning option will get a very good CC, on other occasions, perhaps, not so good. Table 3.12 attempts to be specific.

It must be pointed out that these figures may vary slightly, depending on the number of options involved (see Annex C). It is also true to say that the consensus coefficients of every option will be much reduced, if many voters submit only partial ballots, para 4.5.1. Given their knowledge of the participants and their assessment of just how divisive is the topic in dispute, the consensors may well decide on lower thresholds; whatever their decisions are, they must of course publicise them, prior to the vote.

3.7 Calculating the Exact Outcome

Let us return to Tables 3.7 and 3.8—now combined into Table 3.13—and the associated collective will, Graph 3.8, here repeated as Graph 3.12.

The final outcome was assumed to be 54%. But consider the situation if a fourth voter, a Mr *r*, joins the committee and adds his single-peaked set of preferences,

$$C\text{-}D\text{-}E\text{-}B\text{-}A,$$

Table 3.13 The three voters' rather different preferences and points

Options	The Numbers of Points					MBC score	Consensus Coefficient
	1st = 5 points	2nd = 4 points	3rd = 3 points	4th = 2 points	5th = 1 point		
A				1 = 2	2 = 2	4	0.27
B		1 = 4	1 = 3	1 = 2		9	0.60
C	1 = 5	1 = 4	1 = 3			12	0.80
D	2 =10		1 = 3			13	0.87
E		1 = 4		1 =2	1 = 1	7	0.47

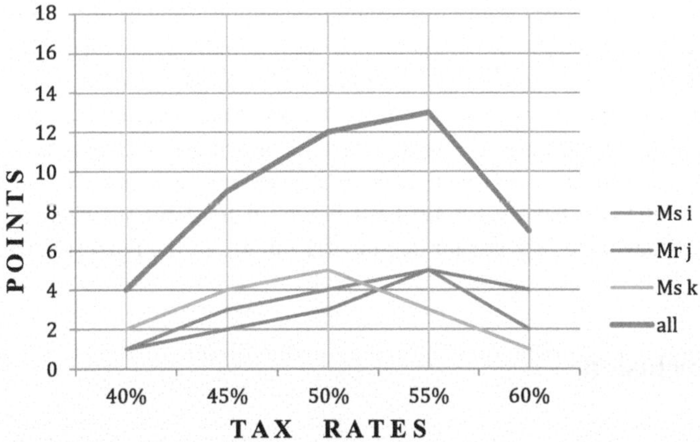

Graph 3.12 The three voters' consensus

Table 3.14 The four voters' preferences and points

Options	The Numbers of Points					MBC score	Consensus Coefficient
	1st	2nd	3rd	4th	5th		
A				1 = 2	3 = 3	5	0.14
B		1 = 4	1 = 3	2 = 4		11	0.55
C	2 = 10	1 = 4	1 = 3			17	0.85
D	2 = 10	1 = 4	1 = 3			17	0.85
E		1 = 4	1 = 3	1 = 2	1 = 1	10	0.50

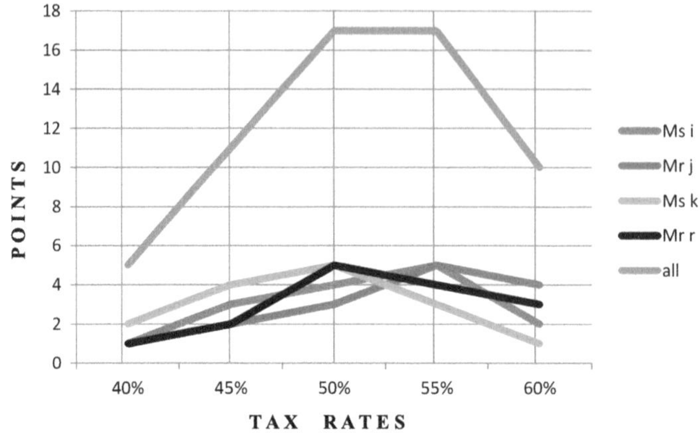

Graph 3.13 The plateau

as shown in Table 3.14.

This would correspond to the collective will shown in Graph 3.13, a plateau. So it's a draw! The two leading options both have a very good CC of 0.85. So here the consensors' decision for the final outcome is obviously going to be a compromise between the two of 52.5%. And given that the plateau is tilted almost symmetrically to options ***B*** and ***E***, maybe the final outcome should indeed be exactly that, 52.5%.

Accordingly, just as individual opinions can be interpreted in many different ways, as per the guidelines in Annex B, so too the final outcome can be analysed, scientifically and accurately, to give a precise identification of the voters' collective will. It only requires the consensors to state, beforehand, whether the final outcome will be resolved to the nearest whole number or, as in this example where any plateau might necessitate a slightly greater degree of accuracy, to the nearest 0.5%.

3.8 Conclusion

Politics, they say, is the art of compromise; consensus voting is indeed its science.

Chapter 4
Consensus Voting

Abstract As it were by definition, when a pluralist democracy has a problem which is complex and/or controversial, achieving unanimity is probably impossible. Such a degree of agreement can definitely not be achieved by distorting the question into an artificial dichotomy, so pitching one side against the other in what then becomes a yes-or-no ballot. If preferential voting is used, however, in which voters do not vote *against* each other, it should be possible for all to have a more rational debate, to exercise a bit of give-and-take and to achieve if not a consensus then at least a best possible compromise.

4.1 Introduction

As is often said in this text, compromise is key to collective decision-making. Politics should not be a series of adversarial win-or-lose contests based on dichotomies; rather, in every debate on matters of contention, and on nearly every decision-making ballot paper, there should invariably be a range of options, so to represent the range of the debate.[1] In other words, ballot papers should always offer at least one compromise option.

As noted in Chap. 2, in a modified Borda count MBC, every voter is encouraged (by the very mathematics of the count) to cast a full slate of preferences. In effect, each can vote for their favourite option, but each may also state their compromise option(s). And sure enough, if everyone does declare their compromise option(s), it should be possible to identify the collective compromise… and the appropriate methodology is indeed the MBC.

In casting a full slate of preferences, in giving some support to the other options, voters accept the judgment of the consensors and recognise the validity of the options listed. Or in other words, every voter as it were acknowledges the aspirations of their neighbours and implies that if indeed one of these options turns out to be the

[1] Just as elections should always offer a range of candidates.

P. Emerson, *Democratic Decision-making*,
SpringerBriefs in Political Science,
https://doi.org/10.1007/978-3-030-52808-9_4

popular will, he/she will abide by this result. In like manner, as was seen in para 2.5.1, the protagonist is also encouraged by the mathematics of the count to be far more positive towards any erstwhile (majoritarian) opponents. Indeed, mindful of the importance of everybody's preferences, it would be to her advantage to draft her proposed option in such a way as to appeal to the broadest possible range of voters. So the protagonists too have to compromise, even prior to the debate. During which, of course, the consensors may well introduce a further element of compromise by asking the movers of two very similar options to form a single composite.

Therefore, in debate, there may be the incentive to compromise. Next, as just noted in the vote itself, voters are encouraged to state their compromise options. While after the vote, in the analysis, if the consensors managed to arrange the options in a spectrum of opinion, and if the two leading options are 'adjacent'—para 3.5—they may well choose to form a final composite—yet another element of compromise.

4.2 The Balanced Debate—the Choice of Options

Debates must be fair. The chair should ensure every option is discussed in equal measure, and the consensors should try to make sure that the list of options is always balanced.[2] When discussing possible tax rates, as we did in Chap. 3, it would have been unwise to reduce everything to a simple '43%, yes-or-no?—the government's choice in para 3.4—partly because a 'yes' cannot be interpreted as definitely demonstrating overwhelming support for this figure of 43%, while a 'no' vote would mean the dispute was still unresolved. The second form of majority voting, an '***X***% or ***Y***%?' question—43 or 56%, to take both government's and opposition's options—would not be much better. Regardless of which is the winner, and regardless of its margin of victory, no one can know for sure whether or not the actual will of those voting is for something a little higher or lower. As shown in the last chapter, however, a multi-option debate can facilitate a very accurate calculation of the collective will.

In para 3.4, the consensors chose the five options—***A***, ***B***, ***C***, ***D*** and ***E***—of 40-45-50-55-60%. If they had settled for a different set of five options, something unbalanced and blatantly biased, like 40-41-42-43-60, the outcome of any vote would almost certainly have been in the lower 40s. The debate, yes, must be balanced (and in 1986, in the first trial of a prototype of the MBC when we debated the constitutional position of Northern Ireland, sure enough, we had some British/Unionist options, some Irish/Nationalist, and one or two which were either neither or both).

[2]In an MBC on five options, four of which are variations on the theme of *x* while only one is of *y* and none is of *z*, then one or other form of *x* is almost bound to win. Some people criticise the Borda methodologies because they are open to such manipulation, but hence, the consensors. *Inter alia*, their job is to ensure that such manipulation is difficult if not indeed impossible.

4.2.1 The Balanced Debate—the Number of Options

Now in the current example of tax rates, we have this range of five of them,

40-45-50-55-60
A-B-C-D-E.

It could just as easily have been six options:

40-44-48-52-56-60
A′-B′-C′-D′-E′-F′.

It is always up to the consensors to decide how many options best represent the debate. In many instances, the minimum should be four and, if the topic is complex, as was said earlier, it's usually best to have a maximum of six.

Suffice here to say that, in the first setting of five balanced options, those who would want a tax rate of 53% could vote:

55-50-45-40-60
D-C-B-A-E

while in the six-option ballot, they might opt for:

52-56-48-60-44-40
D′-E′-C′-F′-B′-A′

In any binary vote, the choice of question can determine literally everything (para 3.2). In consensus voting, insisting on a range of options means that such blatant manipulation is far less likely.

Now it could have been just four options:

$40\text{-}46^{2}/_{3}\text{-}53^{1}/_{3}\text{-}60$

but that would have been a bit messy. It could even have been just three options:

40-50-60

As noted in fn 7 of para 2.4, however, that would obviously have given a huge and totally artificial advantage to the middle option of 50%.

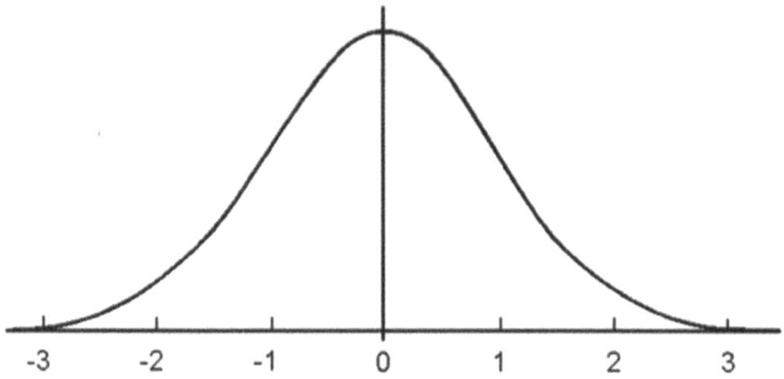

Fig. 4.1 The normal distribution curve

4.3 The Normal Distribution Curve

In many debates, there are those on the left and others on the right. With majority voting, it's just the two options, so debates on tax rates tend to be binary, 'high or low?' for example—56 or 43%—as if there were no compromise. In multi-option voting, the setting may sometimes be compared to a normal distribution curve.

Just as there are quite a few very tall adults in the world, and quite a few very small ones too, most people are somewhere close to the average. In like manner in politics, there are folks on the left wing and others on the right; there are the extremists of both; but the great bulk of opinion is often in the middle.

The art of the consensors is to devise a range of options which covers all the valid proposals raised in the debate, and then to identify—as was mentioned, to the nearest percentage point or whatever—that which best represents the collective will of those voting.

This does not mean that the result of every MBC ballot will be that which is represented by the centre of such a normal distribution curve, as in Fig. 4.1. As the old saying goes, 'there's nought as queer as folks', and on many occasions, opinions will not fit so easily onto such a symmetrical display. Suffice here to say, however, that if a debate is ranged between two extreme positions, the outcome (of any majority vote is almost bound to be wrong, while that) of any MBC ballot will never be either extreme if, that is, the consensors have done a good job.

4.4 The Vote

As was stated in para 2.5.1, the MBC is based on the (*m*, *m*-1 … 1) rule. So the voter who wants to give his favourite the biggest possible number of points, *n*, is thus encouraged to cast all his preferences, even though this means giving 1 point to that option which perhaps he doesn't like at all. But he recognises its validity. And if this last option turns out to be everyone's consensus, then, yes, he implies that he will accept this decision.

The protagonist wants to win, of course. So, as was also stated, she would be well advised to encourage all her supporters to give her favourite option their 1st preference... in *full* ballots. In the hustings, therefore, and on the campaign trail, she will be asked to state her own preferences... and everything becomes much more inclusive. Furthermore, let me say again, it will also be to her advantage to campaign amongst her (erstwhile majoritarian opponents and) other neighbours, so that the latter might also give her option a fairly high preference.

In this way, both voters and protagonists are encouraged to cross the gender gap as well as the party and even the ethno-religious divides. That said, there may well be those occasions when, for reasons of conscience or whatever, some voters might not want to submit a full list of options; suffice here to say that the MBC does not force anyone to do anything, it merely encourages both voters and campaigners to participate in the democratic process and to the full.

4.5 The Count

In theory, in any MBC ballot of n options, every option will be the proposal of at least one voter. Only in a hypothetical situation, therefore, would all v voters give a particular option their 1st preference, so that this option then received the maximum CC of 1.00.

In like manner, in most circumstances, every option will get some support, and nothing will get zero, if only because an option will not be on the ballot paper unless, in debate, it was proposed by one or more of the participants.

So in most situations, every option will get some support. No one option will win everything, and no one option will suffer total ignominy with a CC of 0.00. This takes us back to the normal distribution curve: a collective will is probably somewhere in the middle.

4.5.1 Partial Voting

Unlike the Borda count BC, the MBC encourages the voters to cast a full slate of preferences.[3] But it does not force them to do so. That said, a consensus is more likely to be achieved if voters are acting in a consensual manner, acknowledging their neighbours' aspirations and so on and casting their preferences for all n options.

If every voter does cast a full slate of preferences, the winning option, the one with the highest MBC score, will also have the highest average preference. If, however,

[3]As explained in para 2.5.1, a BC can incentivize the voter to cast only a 1st preference, in other words, to act selfishly.

some of the voters have submitted only partial ballots, then this might not be the case. Obviously, if a whole load of voters cast only a single preference for option ***B***, say, then ***B*** might well get the highest score; it might not, however, pass the minimum CC threshold laid down by the consensors for that outcome to then become binding.

On an initial glance, this might look unfair. As we saw in para 2.5.1, he who casts only a 1st preference gives his favourite just 1 point; she who casts two preferences gives her favourite 2 points; and in a five-option poll, those who cast all five preferences give their favourite the full 5 points.

So he uses just 1 point; she exercises $2 + 1 = 3$ points; and they each get $5 + 4 + 3 + 2 + 1 = 15$ points; that's 15 times as many points as the first guy! Goodness (not badness) me! For the difference however between any voter's 1st preference and their 2nd preference, regardless of whether or not they have cast, that 2nd preference is always 1 point. Indeed, the difference between any voter's (x)th preference and their $(x + 1)$th preference, cast or uncast, is, yes, 1 point.

Now if three voters cast full ballots on five options—the same ***A***, ***B***, ***C***, ***D*** and ***E***—and if, as in para 3.5.2, their preferences are ***D-C-B-E-A***, ***D-E-C-B-A*** and ***C-B-D-A-E***, the results, as shown in Table 3.8, would be ***A*** 4, ***B*** 9, ***C*** 12, ***D*** 13, ***E*** 7, for CCs of 0.27 for CC_A, 0.60 for CC_B, 0.80 for CC_C, 0.87 for CC_D and 0.47 for CC_E. {Add these five CCs and, for three voters, we get $3 \times 1 = 3.0$ (or 3.1, which is as near as damn it).}

If, however, the third voter had submitted a partial ballot with only a 1st preference for option ***C***, then the scores would be ***A*** 2, ***B*** 5, ***C*** 8, ***D*** 10, ***E*** 6, for CCs of 0.13 for CC_A, 0.33 for CC_B, 0.53 for CC_C, 0.67 for CC_D and 0.40 for CC_E. So option ***D*** is still the winner, but with a CC which might not pass the consensors' threshold to be enacted. Furthermore, the ***C*** voter will have done himself no favours: having come a close second when casting a full ballot, he now comes a more distant second.

Now let's look at the two ***D*** supporters, and if they had submitted partial votes of only their 1st preferences, the scores would become ***A*** 2, ***B*** 4, ***C*** 5, ***D*** 5, ***E*** 1, for CCs of 0.13 for CC_A, 0.27 for CC_B, 0.33 for CC_C and CC_D and 0.07 for CC_E. So they too would not have acted in their best interests. Having come top with full ballots, they now come only joint first, with coefficients well below the threshold!

In all, the MBC encourages every voter to submit a full ballot, not only the potential winners but all the participants. If you cast only one preference, you give your 1st preference a 1 point advantage over your 5th preference; and if you cast all five preferences, it gets a four-point advantage. Furthermore, an option's CC is a measure, not only of that option's level of support, but also of the degree to which all the voters have participated in the democratic process. What it does not do is take account of the overall turnout, the percentage of eligible voters who have participated in the voting process.

4.6 The Analysis

The option with the highest score is the result, and this outcome will be binding if its CC is sufficiently high—para 3.6 and Table 3.12. If the outcome is a composite of the two most popular options, the CC of the composite will be higher than that of either. Here, I'm afraid, the mathematics for calculating the composite's CC is beyond the scope of this book (mainly because it is beyond the understanding of this author).

4.7 Manipulation

With the simplest of voting procedures, as in binary voting, it can be quite easy to guesstimate how other people might vote. (This is especially true in an elected parliament, if and when that chamber is majoritarian and if most or all of its members are subject to the various party whips.) It becomes rather more difficult if the votes are free; and it would become extremely difficult if the MPs were to have to work out how the others were going to cast their preferences. Go one step further, and it would be almost impossible to predict the outcome if compositing was also likely.

Furthermore, if an MP votes dishonestly—i.e. if he tries to manipulate things—his preferences will not be single-peaked; and, of course, the votes of any elected representative when exercised in parliament will be—or should be—in the public domain. If lots of MPs act in this way, it might mean the second most popular option is not 'adjacent' to the absolute winner. This might confuse matters when the consensors come to analyse the final results with a view to forming a composite. In other words, in an MBC, MPs should be careful of what they wish for.

4.8 Inter-party Negotiations

In majoritarian politics, those who declare their fallback position have already fallen back to it. So those involved tend to keep their cards close to their chests and inter-party negotiations, not least those on forming coalition governments, can be problematic and protracted.

In consensus politics, there is an altogether different milieu. Those concerned can lay their cards on the table; everyone can know what are the various preferences of all the participants. And consensus voting reaches its fullest potential when, as a result of the procedures for the debate being fully implemented, it gets to the stage when a vote is not really necessary—although it might be helpful to all, if everyone knows the exact levels of support for all the options.

4.9 Conclusion

Everything depends upon the rules of the voting procedure; the atmosphere of any referendum campaign will be determined by the nature of the vote laid down for the conduct of that referendum. With a divisive binary vote, the electorate might well divide or, if the electorate is divided already, the ballot may exacerbate that division.

With consensus voting, there is, yes, an altogether different atmosphere. Nobody votes 'no' against anybody or against anybody's aspiration. Instead, albeit in order of preference, everyone votes 'yes'. Furthermore, as explained above, the voters are encouraged to submit full ballots. And secondly, the protagonists are incentivised to cater for the wishes of more than just their own supporters. The atmosphere is inclusive; the methodology is inclusive; and experience over a number of years shows that, even in conflict zones like Northern Ireland and Bosnia, consensus voting works!

Chapter 5
The Consequences of Consequences

Abstract The modified Borda count (MBC) is more accurate and fairer than majority voting. The former is also non-majoritarian: the MBC can identify that option which has the highest *average* preference... and an average, of course, involves everyone who submits a valid vote, not just a majority of them. If then the MBC were to be the international norm, there would be no further justification for binary majority rule; instead, a different form of governance—'preferential majority rule'—could be based on MBC decision-making in all-party power-sharing coalitions. We now explain how.

5.1 Introduction

In most situations, whenever a serious controversy occurs, unanimity on any one option is improbable if not impossible—that or it's artificial, or fake.[1] Accordingly, given that forms of minority rule absolute monarchies or worse, dictatorships—were and are quite unacceptable, it was felt that the democratic process should seek to identify a majority opinion: the option which brings the greatest good to the greatest number—the superlative of the superlative. Needless to say, this cannot be done well in a process which is only comparative, i.e. with a binary vote. Alas many people think the very opposite: that a *majority* opinion can be identified in a *majority* vote, if not indeed only in a majority vote; it sounds logical, but as we saw in Chap. 2, it is a paradoxical nonsense.

There are in fact numerous ways in which a majority opinion can be identified, as we shall discuss in Chap. 6. As shown in the author's earlier works (Emerson 2012, 2019), the consequences of our ubiquitous obsession with majority voting have often been horrific: everything from the referendums of Napoléon and Hitler, to the practice of majoritarianism in the Soviet Union—the original Russian word is

[1] In Resolution 1441, the UN General Assembly voted, unanimously, on Iraq. Both France and Germany voted in favour, even though neither liked the phrase 'serious consequences'. So why does a country vote in favour of something it does not like? This is yet another restriction of majority voting.

P. Emerson, *Democratic Decision-making*,
SpringerBriefs in Political Science,
https://doi.org/10.1007/978-3-030-52808-9_5

'bolshevism'[2]—to what may be the world's worst instance of binary politics—Máo Zédōng's anti-rightist campaign and the subsequent famine; it was called the Great Leap Forward; it has been estimated it meant death for over 20, maybe even 40 million.

To progress from this divisive form of decision-making to a more accurate—and therefore more democratic—methodology should be an imperative. If we could do this, the consequences could be several. After all, as implied earlier, the MBC encourages the voters to be more thoughtful, the protagonists to be more persuasive and the various supporters to be more accommodating. Replacing the majority vote as the basis of democratic governance would also encourage the politicians to be less adversarial in their day-to-day workings with their parliamentary colleagues. Accordingly, we now consider the advantages of all three consensus voting methodologies—in decision-making, the MBC; in elections, the quota Borda system QBS; and in governance, the matrix vote.

5.2 The MBC

As the reader now knows, the MBC is inclusive and robust, and it can be very accurate. Furthermore, as we saw in para 2.5.1, the very mathematics of an MBC count encourages voters and MPs, in referendums and parliamentary votes respectively, to act in a more co-operative way with their neighbours and/or fellow parliamentarians.

5.3 The Quota Borda System, QBS

The MBC has many qualities, but it is not a system of proportional representation, PR. Accordingly, a quota element has been added to form an electoral system which is indeed proportional: QBS[3] (Dummett 1997: 138 et seq.). Furthermore, its proportionality works on the basis of whatever the voters decide; let me explain. In a PR-list system, seats are awarded to those candidates/parties which receive sufficient support, so proportionality is determined by party affiliations. In QBS (and PR- STV, proportional representation—single transferable vote), the voters themselves decide: so if a quota of voters feel that gender balance, for example, is of overriding importance, and if all of this quota give their 1st and subsequent preferences to, let us say, candidates Ms *t*, Ms *k* and Ms *l*, then, sure enough, at least one of these three will be

[2]It comes from the word *bolshinstvo* meaning majority, and thus the Bolsheviks, while *menshinstvo* means minority and hence the Mensheviks. In the vote which led to the split, in London in 1903, Lenin won by 19 to 17 with 3 abstentions, so he did not have a majority at all, but only the largest minority.

[3]The inventor of this electoral system is the late Professor Sir Michael Dummett, one of the first patrons of the de Borda Institute.

elected. The same principle applies to other policies which may not necessarily be the preserve of only one party, like those on climate change or disarmament.

Proportionality in QBS is much the same, and basically (Emerson 2016: 121), the system works as follows. It is similar to but much easier than PR- STV. The voters cast their preferences, as they wish: in PR- STV, if they want to cast preferences for every candidate, they can do so, even though there is often no point at all in so doing; in QBS, the voters cast up to a fixed number, *n*, preferences—and the usual maximum is six; but the main difference is that while PR- STV allows the voters to cross the party divide, QBS actually encourages them to do so.

In a PR-STV count, there may be eliminations to execute or surpluses to reallocate, fractions of votes to be transferred and decimal places to compound and confuse… but not in QBS. In its simplest form, QBS is like this: in, say, a four-seater constituency, any candidates who get a quota of 1st preferences are elected—that's stage (i); if seats are still to be filled, we move to stage (ii), and if any pair of candidates[4] gets two quotas of 1st/2nd preferences, then both of them get elected; in a final stage, if seats are still to be filled, these are awarded to those candidates with the highest MBC scores.

Ideally, QBS would be used in six-seater constituencies,[5] in which case, the procedure can be a little more complicated but basically, it works on the same principles. The count starts as follows:

- by calculating the quota: that whole number which is greater than V (the valid vote) divided by (*n*, the number of seats + 1)[6]; and then
- by collating

  all the candidates' 1st preference scores;
  all the pairs of candidates' 1st/2nd preference totals; and
  all the candidates' MBC scores.

The count proceeds in two parts, and four stages, and moves to the next part and/or stage, if seats remain to be filled.

Part I

stage (i) all candidates gaining at least one quota of 1st preferences are deemed elected;
stage (ii) both candidates of all pairs gaining at least two quotas of 1st/2nd preferences are deemed elected.

---

[4]If x voters give a 1st preference to candidate *m* and their 2nd preference to candidate *k*,
if y voters give a 1st preference to candidate *k* and their 2nd preference to candidate *m*, and.
if the *k/m* pair, $x + y \geq 2$ quotas,
then both *k* and *m* get elected.

[5]If, as is the case in Ireland, the PR- STV constituencies vary in size (from three- to five-seaters), there should also be a regional or national top-up based, it is suggested, on the parties' MBC totals. With QBS (or PR- STV), if all the constituencies are six-seaters, there is no need for a top-up.

[6]If the number of voters is *V*, and the number of seats to be filled is *n*, then the Droop quota is based on $V/(n + 1)$ and the Hare quota formula on V/n. (See also footnote 5, para 7.2.2.).

Part II (these calculations involve only those candidates as yet unelected)

stage (iii) if any pair of candidates gets at least one quota of 1st/2nd preferences, then the candidate with the higher MBC score gets elected; and finally

stage (iv) seats are awarded to those candidates with the highest MBC scores.

5.3.1 *The Mathematics of* QBS

To get elected, a candidate needs either a good score of top preferences and/or a good MBC score. So, as in the MBC, so too in QBS, the very mathematics of the count encourages the voters to cast a full slate of preferences—in an n-seater constituency where $n < 7$, the rules should ask the voter to list n candidates.

A further advantage of QBS must be mentioned. In Part I stage (i), as noted above, success depends on a quota of 1st preferences. If any one party thinks it has two quotas worth of support, it should best stand two candidates; if it stands only one, it will lose its second seat; if it stands say four candidates, it might split the vote, with each candidate getting only half a quota, so none of them would get elected, at least not at this initial stage. So (unlike some PR-list systems, both PR-STV and) QBS actually encourage the parties to be realistic about the number of candidates they actually nominate.[7]

In campaigning for a good score of 1st preferences, a candidate might concentrate on his/her own immediate supporters. In seeking a good MBC score however, and this might be crucial in Part II of the count, support from across the board might well be vital. Accordingly, as with the MBC, candidates and parties will find it in their best interests to campaign across the entire constituency, and both will be incentivised to co-operate across the party divide.[8]

5.4 The Matrix Vote

The democratic process allows for change. Thus, in many societies, elections are held, every so often (under one system or another—see Chap. 7) and all is done in an open and transparent process—or that's the idea. If and when no one party or no one coalition of two or three parties has a majority of the seats, some countries

[7]In a divided society, as was the case in Bosnia, a six-seater constituency might be 30:30:30 Catholic:Moslem:Orthodox, so any one group might expect two or at most three seats. Doubtless there are the inevitable internal party rivalries; it would nevertheless be unwise for a particular religious group to have four or more candidates. Yet the electorate is asked to fill in six preferences. In this way, at best, voters may be encouraged—not forced, just encouraged—to cross not only the gender gap and any party divides, but maybe too one or perhaps more of the inter-religious chasms.

We are often told that the democratic process is a vital part of the peace process; the voting procedures which form part of that process, therefore, should also be peaceful. QBS fits the bill.

[8]As will be seen in Chap. 7, this quality is shared by the alternative vote, AV.

give some bonus seats to the ‘winner’ so that the winners then do win and by a comfortable margin.[9] In other jurisdictions, politics goes into limbo as their open and transparent elections are followed by, at best, closed and opaque negotiations. In a nutshell, the newly elected members of parliament close the door, draw the curtains and go upstairs, so to concoct a majority. And the gloves are off.

CIRCLE	Minority, one party
DIAMOND	Minority coalition
STAR	Majority, one party
TRIANGLE	Majority coalition
SQUARE	Grand coalition
LINE	Undecided

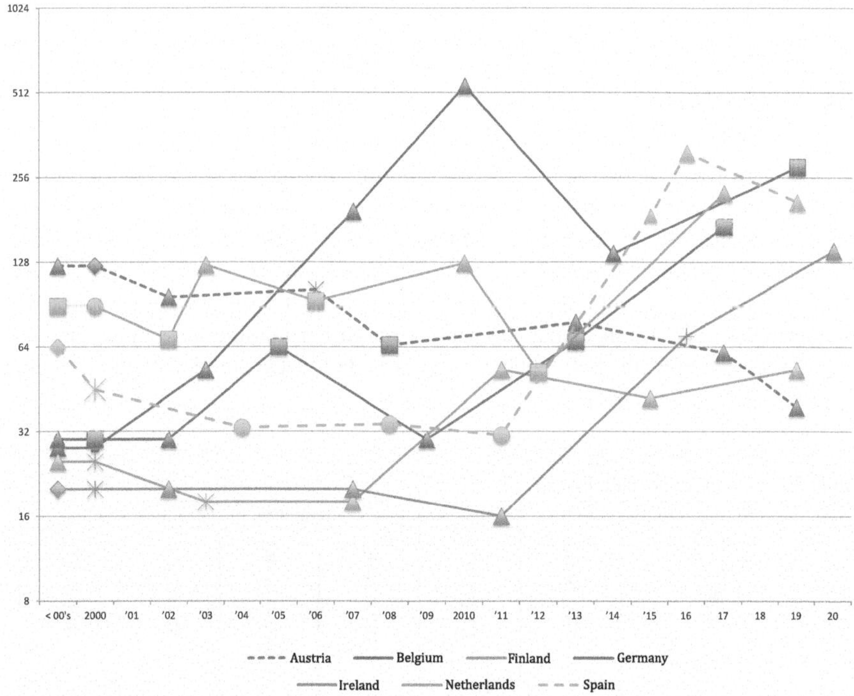

Fig. 5.1 Days, weeks, months…

[9]Greece and Italy, for example. This means, of course, that what had been PR is no longer proportional.

In many multi-party democracies—as in the Netherlands, for example, where in the parliamentary elections of 2017, the various parties finished with 33, 20, 19, 19, 14, 14, 9, 5, 5, 4, 3, 3 and 2 seats in the 150-member chamber—the number of combinations which could be devised to form a majority of 76 where numerous and for some, including this author, countless. No wonder they took quite a long time to sort something out: 225 days. The world record is held by Belgium: 541 days, in 2010/11, but as Fig. 5.1 shows, quite a few other countries are competing for the title, not least Israel where, as I write, three elections and 400 days of negotiations have led to a power-sharing arrangement… which *may* be stable. Some hope.

However, as we saw in Chap. 1, majority voting is not very good. An MBC would be better. The latter is non-majoritarian. Therefore, if adopted, there would be no further justification for binary majority rule. Instead, governance could be based on all-party coalitions. So, the democratic process could be in two phases:

- the people elect the parliament, ideally in a preferential and proportional vote (PR-STV or, better still) QBS; and then
- the parliament could elect the government, ideally in another preferential and proportional vote; this one is called a matrix vote.

5.4.1 The Task

To elect a government, parliament needs to choose a number of MPs to form a cabinet, one MP to be the prime minister, another the minister of finance, another to look after foreign affairs and so on. The talents required for each posting may vary considerably. Accordingly, the ballot paper should be two-dimensional: so, every MP may choose, in order of preference, not only those whom she wishes to be in government, but also the particular portfolio in which she wants each of her nominees to serve. To use a very simple example, the ballot paper for a cabinet of just six ministers, those named in Table 5.1, might suffice.

Table 5.1 A matrix vote ballot paper

The Cabinet		Prime Minister	Ministers of….				
Preference	Name		Climate Change	Disarmament	Environment	Agriculture	Education
1st							
2nd							
3rd							
4th							
5th							
6th							

Table 5.2 A semi-completed matrix vote ballot

The Cabinet		Prime Minister	Ministers of....				
Preference	Name		Climate Change	Disarmament	Environment	Agriculture	Education
1st	Mr *l*		✓				
2nd	Ms *p*				✓		
3rd	Ms s	✓					
4th	Ms *q*						✓
5th	Mr *o*					✓	
6th	Mr *j*			✓			

5.4.2 A Simple Matrix Vote

It's all fairly straightforward. Every MP chooses those six MPs whom she wants to be in cabinet; so let's take the situation for Ms *p*, a newly elected MP for the multi-seat constituency of somewhere. Her first priority might well be climate change, and if Mr *l* is her nominee, then he gets her 1st preference. The environment is also a major concern, and here she wants to propose herself. Her 3rd preference is for Ms *s* to be the prime minister, PM; in a consensual polity, it's maybe not the most important post, but determining the consensus of any multi-party cabinet does require considerable skills. And so on: her other nominees are: 4th, Ms *q* for education; 5th, Mr *o* for agriculture; and 6th, Mr *j* for disarmament.

Accordingly, her completed ballot paper could be as shown in Table 5.2: one tick in each column and one in each row. In the count, it will be read as a 1st preference for Mr *l*, and (because she cast all six preferences) he thus gets 6 points for the post of climate change; a 2nd preference for herself, Ms *p*, she gets 5 points for the environment portfolio, and so on.

5.4.3 The Count

A matrix vote count consists of two phases (Emerson 2016: 82 et seq.). The first is a QBS election, an analysis of all the data in the shaded part of the ballots, as in Table 5.2, so to identify the six most popular MPs, and these shall form the cabinet. In phase two, each of these six shall be appointed to the portfolio for which they have the most points, so this phase is an MBC analysis of the data in the matrix itself.

A hypothetical example of a 50-member parliament electing a six-member cabinet is shown in Table 5.3. Each MP submits a ballot of six preferences, so each is an allocation of $6 + 5 + 4 + 3 + 2 + 1 = 21$ points; so, with full ballots from every MP,

Table 5.3 A matrix vote tally

The Cabinet		Prime Minister	Ministers of....					MBC scores
			Climate Change	Disarmament	Environment	Agriculture	Education	
Preference	Name							
1st	Ms p		40		200		40	280
2nd	Mr q	20	160	10	20			210
3rd	Ms r	140		20			20	180
4th	Mr s			20		140		160
= 5th	Ms t	20		80		10		110
= 5th	Mr u			20		10	80	110
	MBC scores		200	150	220	160	140	1,050

the total number of points is $50 \times 21 = 1050$. In a nutshell, all the points cast are added together to see which candidates get the biggest sums and for which ministries, and in the right-hand column, to see which get the highest scores. (Needless to say, the MBC social ranking may not be exactly the same as that of the QBS analysis: if you use a slightly different counting procedure, you might get a slightly different answer.)

The candidate with the highest sum is the first to be appointed to the portfolio indicated, and so on, in descending order. In the event of a tie, priority is given to the more popular candidate (as measured in the QBS election) and/or the more contested ministerial post.

In the example shown, the two top scores are 200 and 160, so these see the appointment of our first voter Ms *p* to the environment and Mr *q* to climate change. Next comes a tie—140, and there are two of them, shown in a dark tint; but there's no clash, Ms *r* becomes PM, and Mr *s* takes on agriculture. With 80, in a lighter tint, there is another tie, and both MPs are equally popular in the QBS count (and on MBC scores of 110); but disarmament gets a higher MBC score than does education, so Ms t gets the former and Mr *u* the latter, in that order. The final result is shown in Table 5.4.

5.4.4 *The Tactics*

QBS is PR. If party ***W*** has 40% of a parliament, it can expect about 40% of the cabinet, so for a 6-person executive, it might well get two or even three ministerial posts. Party ***X*** on 30% should get two. Party ***Y*** with just 20% might get only one minister. While party ***Z*** on only 10% of the MPs will probably get no seats at all… unless, of course, it co-operates with one of the bigger parties.

Table 5.4 A matrix vote result

The Cabinet		Ministers of...						MBC scores
Preference	Name	Environment	Climate Change	Prime Minister	Agriculture	Disarmament	Education	
1st	Ms p	200						280
2nd	Mr q		160					210
3rd	Ms r			140				180
4th	Mr s				140			160
= 5th	Ms t					80		110
= 5th	Mr u						80	110
	MBC scores	220	200	180	160	150	140	1,050

As we now know, the MBC element of the vote encourages every MP to submit a full ballot of six preferences. And, para 5.3, QBS suggests every party should nominate only as many candidates as it thinks it will get elected; so, they choose their best, for ministerial posts for which (supposedly) they have the talent: so, ***W*** nominates 3 or 4 at the most, ***X*** has 2 or maybe even 3, ***Y*** probably has 2 and ***Z*** just the 1. If then the MPs all submit full ballots, every MP will cross the party divide—and this minimal degree of co-operation should surely be an essential feature of any power-sharing arrangement.

5.4.5 A Real Matrix Vote

In practice, of course, life is not so simple. Lots of MPs will want their party leader to be the PM; none of them would trust a voting procedure which had the potential to ditch their leader into oblivion. Accordingly, the actual procedure allows the voter to cast three priorities—P_1, P_2 and P_3—and it's (not a tick but) a P_1 in each column and a P_1 in each row. (The P_2's and P_3's can be anywhere.) If, then, a candidate with a P_1 to be the PM does not get that post, that preference will be transferred to the voter's P_2. And the count continues.

Logically, therefore, it is well worth giving your 1st preference not just a P_1 but a P_2 and maybe a P_3 as well. But it's probably not worth the effort for your bottom preferences. Instead of that which is shown in Table 5.2, a completed ballot will look like that depicted in Table 5.5, with all the 1st priorities, the P_1's, shown in tint.

And don't forget, the matrix vote is for use in parliament. It might look a little complicated, but there are only a few hundred MPs, and these people are meant to be clever. Furthermore, the whole thing can be done electronically. Later on, if a cabinet minister dies or absconds, the procedure is a recount, with the deceased no longer a participant, and subsequent preferences/priorities now taking precedence. For most

Table 5.5 A fully completed matrix vote ballot

The Cabinet		Ministers of....					
Preference	Name	Prime Minister	Climate Change	Disarmament	Environment	Agriculture	Education
1st	Mr *l*		P_1	P_3	P_2		
2nd	Ms *p*		P_2		P_1		P_3
3rd	Ms s	P_1				P_3	P_2
4th	Ms *q*					P_2	P_1
5th	Mr *o*					P_1	
6th	Mr *j*			P_1			

members of cabinet, any one death or resignation will probably involve just a minor reshuffle.

A matrix vote may also be used whenever a group of persons want to elect a fixed number of individuals to form a committee, a cabinet, an executive or a team—a group in which each has a different function but in which all co-operate. Examples are legion: an association electing its executive at an AGM; party members electing their national executive at an annual conference; the MPs of two or more parties choosing a power-sharing majority coalition government; the fans of a football club selecting their first XI; and so on.

5.5 Conclusion

So, the full basis of a power-sharing democracy is as follows, and we now add a third feature:

- the people elect the parliament, ideally in a preferential and proportional vote, PR-STV or, better still QBS; next
- the parliament elects the government, ideally in another preferential and proportional vote, a matrix vote; and then
- policies shall be ratified (or not, as the case may be) in preferential MBC ballots.

One inevitable consequence is that the party whip will be less powerful if not indeed obsolescent. In majority voting, it's 'this' or 'that' but, as we saw in para 2.5, consensus voting offers much greater choice. In a six-option MBC ballot, there are, yes, 720 different ways of voting (and it would be very difficult for any party whip to say that one set of preferences is correct and all the other 719 are not). In a matrix vote, there is even more choice: the MP may choose any one of say 20 MPs to be any one of six ministers; next, any one of 19 MPs to be one of the remaining 5 ministers; and so on. In all, each MP shall have the opportunity to vote in over 20,000,000,000 different ways. In a parliament of hundreds electing a cabinet of a dozen or more, the degree of choice is enormous; if each has a lot of choices, the degree to which any PM can control things is of course much reduced. Indeed, in such a setting, it would be almost impossible to control. Instead, as always in consensus voting, nobody wins everything, no one controls anything, but (almost) everyone wins something.

Will it work? Firstly, let it be emphasised that majority voting does not work well or even, in the worst cases, at all; as in the Balkans and elsewhere, it has sometimes been the catalyst of wars. Secondly, having all-powerful but divisive individuals—presidents and/or prime ministers, the likes of Bolsonaro, Erdoğan, Johnson, Modi, Netanyahu, Orban, Putin and Trump—is not good for *Homo sapiens*, let alone the environment. To tackle the problems of climate change or COVID-19 requires everyone to work together: governments of national unity, working in consensus. I rest my case.

References

Dummett, M. (1997). *Principles of electoral reform*. Oxford: Oxford University Press.
Emerson, P. (2012). *Defining democracy*. Heidelberg: Springer.
Emerson, P. (2016). *From majority rule to inclusive politics*. Heidelberg: Springer.
Emerson, P. (2020). *Majority voting as a catalyst of populism*. Heidelberg: Springer.

Chapter 6
Comparing Decision-Making Voting Procedures

Abstract There are, of course, lots of different ways of voting and, therefore, for some voters' profiles, lots of different analyses. They can't all be right. And yet, for some extraordinary reason, nearly all of these voting procedures are regarded as democratic. A change of procedure, however, might mean a completely different result. So this chapter will examine and compare the most common forms of decision-making, so to determine which (if any) are useless, which mediocre and which are accurate.

6.1 Introduction—A Little History

Not least because majority voting is so inadequate, there have been many attempts at devising alternative methodologies—the first was nearly 2000 years ago, by Pliny the Younger, (para 1.3.2); the second was, I think, a plurality vote nearly 1000 years ago in China (Franke and Twitchett 1994: 266).

Now of course, non-binary decision-making voting systems can be used only if there are more than two options on the table... and on the ballot paper! These voting mechanisms vary enormously. Some allow the voter to choose only one option, others are more inclusive, a few are preferential; and taken together, they include the following:

Single preference voting procedures:

Plurality voting
The two-round system, TRS
Serial voting.

Multi-option voting:

Approval voting
Range voting.

P. Emerson, *Democratic Decision-making*,
SpringerBriefs in Political Science,
https://doi.org/10.1007/978-3-030-52808-9_6

Table 6.1 20 voters' 1st preferences

	No. of Voters				
	6	5	4	3	2
1st preference	*A*	*E*	*C*	*D*	*B*

Preferential voting:

The alternative vote, AV[1]
A Borda count, BC and a modified BC, the MBC
The Condorcet rule.

6.2 The Practice

Comparing the accuracy of different decision-making systems—from binary voting to preferential—is relatively easy. Consider, for example, a democratic society in England in 2016, of just 20 voters, preparing to make a decision about Brexit. There were lots of options: option ***A***, the UK in the EU; option ***B***, the UK in the EEA; option ***C***, in a customs union; option ***D***, the single market; ***E***, under the WTO[2] (and lots of variations on these various themes). And let us assume our score of voters have mixed opinions, as in Table 6.1.

For those who believe that politics should be majoritarian, there is no majority *in favour of* any one option so, as we saw in Chap. 1, the corollary is also true: there is a majority *against* every goddamned option. Little wonder then that the political arguments on Brexit were so adversarial.

But back to the theory and, as in the example of the Pink Party, given the obvious limitations of majority voting, an accurate assessment of the above 20 voters' collective opinion is more likely to be achieved by an analysis of their preferences.

Some political problems can indeed be really divisive, and Brexit was exactly that. But the UK had a binary vote only on option ***A***, whether or not the UK should remain in the EU. As noted in the footnote of para 2.1.1, only *afterwards* was there a debate, or rather a bloody great row, about all the other options. Consider, then, the hypothetical voters' profile, in which 20 voters have different opinions, as in Table 6.2.

Opinions, it seems, are really divided. The first six voters have the complete opposite set of preferences to the next five—***A-B-C-D-E*** as opposed to ***E-D-C-B-A***—while the other nine voters don't like either ***A*** or ***E***.

[1]In Britain and Ireland, this is also called the single transferable vote, STV, and in its PR format, it's used in Ireland, North and South, as PR-STV. In North America, it is instant run-off voting, IRV. And when used in decision-making in Australasia, it is preferential voting or PV.

[2]EU, The European Union; EEA, the European Economic Area; WTO, the World Trade Organisation.

Table 6.2 The 20 voters' profile

Preferences	No. of Voters				
	6	5	4	3	2
1st	***A***	***E***	***C***	***D***	***B***
2nd	***B***	***D***	***B***	***C***	***D***
3rd	***C***	***C***	***D***	***B***	***A***
4th	***D***	***B***	***E***	***E***	***E***
5th	***E***	***A***	***A***	***A***	***C***

Table 6.3 The 21 voters' profile

Preferences	No. of Voters					
	6	5	4	3	2	1
1st	***A***	***E***	***C***	***D***	***B***	***F***
2nd	***B***	***D***	***B***	***C***	***D***	-
3rd	***C***	***C***	***D***	***B***	***A***	-
4th	***D***	***B***	***E***	***E***	***E***	-
5th	***E***	***A***	***A***	***A***	***C***	-
6th	***F***	***F***	***F***	***F***	***F***	-

6.2.1 Another Opinion

Now add to the fray another voter, just one, who is convinced that everyone should just forget about Europe and that, instead, the UK should become the 51st state of the USA. The 20 voters think this last option is bizarre, but it's legal, and it's therefore possible (although highly improbable), but let us assume that the consensors agree to add it to the ballot paper. The new voters' profile is shown in Table 6.3.

On the face of it, ***F*** is an absolute no–no, while opinions on ***A*** and ***E*** are indeed very polarised. So maybe ***B***, ***C*** or ***D*** best represent the 21 voters' collective will. Well, let's have a look and see what happens if these 21 persons decide to resolve the problem, democratically, i.e. with a vote.

6.2.2 The Analyses

Plurality voting With plurality voting, only the 1st preferences cast are taken into consideration, so the social ranking is ***A-E-C-D-B-F***, so the winner, the social choice, is option ***A*** on a score of 6.

TRS In TRS, because no one option gets a majority in the first round, a second-round majority vote is held between the two leading options, in this case ***A*** and ***E***. In which case, if everyone's preferences stay the same, option ***E*** wins by 12–8.

Serial voting Serial voting, a series of majority votes, is usually used when debating amendments: the options are listed in order—in this instance, a pro- to anti-EU order of ***A-B-C-D-E–F***—and majority votes are taken between the two extreme options until, as in musical chairs, only one remains. ***A*** beats ***F***, the loser is eliminated, and it's now ***A-B-C-D-E***. ***E*** beats ***A***, to produce ***B-C-D-E***. Then it's ***B-C-D*** and ***B-C*** for a final winner of ***C***. Serial voting gives success to the Condorcet winner… if there is one.

Approval voting Approval voting may be interpreted in a number of ways: by regarding all 1st and 2nd preferences, or maybe a larger set, as 'approvals', with each cast preference being of equal value. So, counting

1st and 2nd preferences,	***B*** wins on 12;
1st, 2nd and 3rd's,	***C*** tops the scores on 18;
1st, 2nd, 3rd and 4th's,	it's a ***B/D*** draw;
1st, 2nd, 3rd, 4th and 5th's,	all ***A, B, C, D*** and ***E*** tie on 20; and.
All six preferences,	the winner is ***F*** on 21!

But that's crazy. Twenty people regard this option as the very worst. Only one guy thinks it deserves any consideration. And it wins! Range voting can produce even more weird results. Furthermore, approval and range voting both encourage intransigence, the latter even more than the former.

AV AV is another knockout system, a series of plurality votes and, after each round, the option with the lowest score is eliminated, with its votes going to its voters' 2nd or subsequent preferences. With a stage (i) score line of ***A***-6, ***E***-5, ***C***-4, ***D***-3, ***B***-2, ***F***-1, ***F*** is out, and there's no change, so ***B*** is out as well, and its two votes go to ***D*** for a stage (iii) score line of ***A***-6, ***E***-5, ***C***-4, ***D***-5. ***C*** is the next one to go, and its four votes go (not to ***B*** which has been eliminated, but) to ***D***, for a new score line of ***A***-6, ***E***-5, ***D***-9, so there's still no option with a majority. Hence, option ***E*** is now withdrawn, and its five votes go to ***D*** for a final score of ***A***-6, ***D***-14, so the AV social choice is option ***D*** on 14.

BC In a BC, on n options, a voter may cast m preferences, where needless to say, $n \geq m \geq 1$ (para 2.5.1). Points are awarded to (1st, 2nd … last) preferences cast according to an (n, n-1 … 1) or an (n-1, n-2 … 0) rule, so in a BC, option ***F*** might well get a full 6 or 5 points; in this respect, a BC is a bit like approval voting, and it also encourages intransigence. Using the (n, n-1 … 1) rule, the BC social ranking is ***B***-89, ***C***-87, ***D***-87, ***E***-69, ***A***-68, ***F***-26, and the social choice is ***B***.

MBC {As noted in para 2.5.1, however, Jean-Charles de Borda implied that points should be awarded in accordance with an (m, m-1 … 1) formula and not an (n, n-1 … 1) and certainly not an (n-1, n-2 … 0) rule; the latter cannot distinguish between a voter's penultimate and her last preference.} Accordingly, in an MBC, if the voter has cast a full ballot, a 1st preference gets 6 points, a 2nd gets 5, a 3rd 4 and so on. If, however, like the ***F*** supporter, he has cast only one preference, then ***F*** gets just 1 point. So the MBC social ranking is ***B***-89, ***C***-87, ***D***-87, ***E***-69, ***A***-68, ***F***-21 so the social choice is still ***B***.

Table 6.4 The outcomes

Methodology		Social Choice	Social Ranking					
Majority voting	"*X*?"	nothing	nothing					
	"*X* or *Y*?"	anything but ***F***	a paradox: ***B*** > ***D*** = ***C*** > ***B*** >...					
Plurality voting		***A***	***A*** 6	***E*** 5	***C*** 4	***D*** 3	***B*** 2	***F*** 1
TRS		***E***	***E*** 12	***A*** 8	-	-	-	-
Serial voting		***C***	***C*** 12	***B*** 8	***D***	***E***	***A***	***F***
Approval voting		***F***	***F*** 21	***A/B/C/D/E*** 20				
Range voting		anything at all	anything					
AV		***D***	***D*** 14	***A*** 6	-	-	-	-
BC		***B***	***B*** 89	***C/D*** 87		***E*** 69	***A*** 68	***F*** 26
MBC		***B***	***B*** 89	***C/D*** 87		***E*** 69	***A*** 68	***F*** 21
Condorcet rule		***C***	***C*** 4.5	***B*** 4	***D*** 3.5	***E*** 2	***A*** 1	***F*** 0

Condorcet With Condorcet, the score line of pairings is ***C***-4.5, ***B***-4, ***D***-3.5, ***E***-2, ***A***-1, ***F***-0, and the social choice is again ***C***. The summary of all these results is in Table 6.4.

So, considering all the different forms of decision-making, majority voting produces either nothing or a paradox. And when comparing the other methodologies, the answer could be ***A*** or ***B*** or ***C*** or ***D*** or ***E*** or ***F***; it could be any damned thing; and all of these outcomes could be regarded as only *totally democratic*. Well, obviously, they can't all be right.

Table 6.5 A comparison

<table>
<tr><th colspan="2" rowspan="2">Decision-making System</th><th rowspan="2">Single or multi preference</th><th colspan="2">As used in decision-making in:</th><th colspan="4">Classification
1 = terrible
2 = bad
3 = so-so
4 = good</th></tr>
<tr><th>Referendums</th><th>Parliaments</th><th>1</th><th>2</th><th>3</th><th>4</th></tr>
<tr><td rowspan="2">Binary voting</td><td>"X, yes - or-no?</td><td>single</td><td rowspan="2">A few countries, e.g., Australia, Ireland, Switzerland,[a] USSR, Venezuela</td><td>Pretty well everywhere, from the DPRK to the USA</td><td>✓</td><td></td><td></td><td></td></tr>
<tr><td>"X or Y?"</td><td>single</td><td>Germany: constructive[b]</td><td></td><td>✓</td><td></td><td></td></tr>
<tr><td colspan="2">Plurality voting</td><td>single</td><td></td><td>Denmark[c]</td><td></td><td>✓</td><td></td><td></td></tr>
<tr><td colspan="2">TRS</td><td>single</td><td>Guam, New Zealand, Sweden</td><td>Norway, though only once, in 1972.</td><td></td><td colspan="2">✓</td><td></td></tr>
<tr><td colspan="2">Serial voting</td><td>single</td><td></td><td>Finland, Sweden</td><td></td><td></td><td>✓</td><td></td></tr>
<tr><td colspan="2">Approval voting</td><td>multi</td><td></td><td></td><td></td><td colspan="2">✓</td><td></td></tr>
<tr><td colspan="2">Range voting</td><td>multi</td><td></td><td></td><td colspan="2">✓</td><td></td><td></td></tr>
<tr><td colspan="2">AV</td><td>multi</td><td></td><td></td><td></td><td></td><td>✓</td><td></td></tr>
<tr><td colspan="2">BC</td><td>multi</td><td></td><td>(Once in DCC.[d])</td><td></td><td colspan="2">✓</td><td></td></tr>
<tr><td colspan="2">MBC</td><td>multi</td><td></td><td></td><td></td><td></td><td></td><td>✓</td></tr>
<tr><td colspan="2">Condorcet</td><td>multi</td><td></td><td></td><td></td><td></td><td></td><td>✓</td></tr>
</table>

[a]Their first was in 1294
[b]See fn 2 of para 1.3.2
[c]The Danish parliament's plurality voting is listed as bad… but it's a darn site better than the simple majority voting which is the norm in most other parliaments
[d]Dublin City Council

Initially, para 6.2.1, it was thought that maybe ***B*** or ***C*** or ***D*** best represents the collective will, and this analysis suggests the answer does indeed lie with some form of preferential voting: AV, BC, MBC or Condorcet. AV, however, can be very capricious; indeed, anything which relies on plurality voting—TRS is the other one—might be unreliable. So the answer is either the MBC and/or the Condorcet rule. A comparison of all these decision-making systems is shown in Table 6.5.

6.3 Summary

At least in this setting (and as explained in Chap. 1), (simple or weighted) binary voting is totally inappropriate for it could produce either nothing… or anything. In multi-option decision-making, single-preference systems are also Orwellian in their simplicity, so little wonder that plurality voting and TRS are often inaccurate. AV is rather better, not least because it encourages some co-operation between the protagonists. So the best methodology, it would seem, is either an MBC and/or the Condorcet rule.

It's again a bit like a sports competition, para 3.1. With six teams in a tournament ***A***, ***B***, ***C***, ***D***, ***E*** and ***F***, there could be two first-round matches allowing for two teams to get byes into the semi-finals, so a lot would depend on the draw! It would of course be better to have a league system: allow each team to play each other, and see which team wins the most matches (Condorcet pairings) or which gets the best goal difference (MBC scores—well, sort of). In most seasons, the champion (Condorcet winner) is also the top goal scorer (MBC winner), and either system is very accurate. Accordingly, on really important issues—in parliamentary votes and so on—a decision should be taken only if the Condorcet social choice coincides with the MBC winner.

6.4 Conclusion

In practice, in most countries, the decision-making system of choice is invariably the binary vote. Was it chosen? Or was it just assumed that, in a democracy, decisions have to be taken in a (simple, weighted or consociational) majority vote. Those involved sometimes argue about minimum turnout requirements, about whether or not the outcome should be binding, or whatever… but seldom do they consider the merits of non-binary and therefore multi-option let alone preferential decision-making.

Furthermore, politicians invariably choose that which is in their vested interest. Sadly, human rights lawyers and even academics rarely compare the various methodologies' democratic credentials.

In the above comparison at least, and maybe too in many other voters' profiles, when compared on a scale of accuracy, the most accurate decision-making system is either the Condorcet and/or the MBC. After that it's Scandinavian serial voting and Denmark's plurality voting, in that order. The rest, as stated, are sometimes just hopelessly inaccurate.

They are shown—or most of them are shown—in Table 6.6. From left-to-right, the x-axis shows the ever-increasing degree of choice available to the voter, while the y-axis indicates the number of preferences cast that will actually be counted.

In theory, then, the x-axis starts with binary voting: either 'Option ***X***, yes-or-no?' questions—the sort which formed the basis of yesterday's votes of Napoléon and Lenin (para 5.1) or today's Brexit ballot (para 6.2)—and/or those of the 'Option ***X*** or option ***Y***?' variety. Both are in the bottom left-hand corner. Now obviously, if the voters cast only a single preference, only their 1st preferences can be counted. Whereas, sure enough, if voters cast some or lots of preferences, then some or all can be taken into account. Table 6.6 therefore has a natural diagonal, with some pretty terrible voting procedures in the bottom left-hand corner, some mediocre in the middle and a few rather good measures of collective will in the top-right corner.

Next comes plurality voting, which is often seen in the Danish parliament and in the first round of some TRS referendums: some of the latter have offered three options, as in Newfoundland, four in Australia, five in New Zealand and six or seven in Guam—their 1982 referendum had six options and one further option left blank, so anyone(s) wishing to (campaign and) vote for a seventh option could do exactly that.

Quite a lot of choice is offered in approval and range voting in which, if everyone is being nice and conciliatory and voting for more than one option, might produce a sort of consensus. As noted, however, those who are intransigent can remain so; indeed, these two procedures actually encourage them to be so. Hence, in Table 6.6, its bandwidth is quite large.

The BC is included. If, as we said in para 6.3, the (n, n-1 ...1) or (n-1, n-2 ... 0) formula is used, and if there are no rules to cover partial voting, then a BC can be as bad as an approval vote.

In theory, the best systems will be those which allow the voters to cast as many preferences as they may wish to, and for all preferences cast by all to be considered in the count. Alas, in AV, some of the preferences cast may actually be ignored, so it's not very accurate; furthermore, AV is like a series of plurality votes, and if the latter are no good, then the former is also going to be a bit dodgy.

The two best systems, then, are the MBC and the Condorcet rule: as we now know, the first is a points system, the second is based on pairings, and they are both very accurate. If we want to see which of five teams is the best, or which of five policies is the most popular, we could have a binary process—a knockout competition in which some teams play two matches but others have to play three (so that's a bit unfair); or we could have a league so that every team plays every other team. With each match a pairing, the champion can be either the team which wins the most matches (Condorcet) and/or the one with the best goal difference (MBC). In 2019/20, up to the time when coronavirus stopped play, Liverpool had won the most matches, and also scored the most goals; so, based on this analysis, Borda or Condorcet, Merseyside would be the champions.

Table 6.6 Decision-making

		CLOSED QUESTIONS		SEMI-OPEN QUESTIONS	OPEN QUESTIONS	
↑	All preferences					MBC Condorcet
C O	many preferences some preferences a few preferences			Approval & Range Voting; BC		BC AV, IRV, PV r STV
U				TRS Norway New Zealand (referendums)	*Serial Voting* Sweden	
N	1st preferences only	Weighted Finland, SA Qualified EU	Consociational Belgium NI			
T		Simple Majority Poland, UK	Twin Majority Switzerland (referendums)	Plurality Vote Denmark		
		1 of 2 options		1 of some options	1 or some of all options	1 or some or all of all options
		1st preference only			preferential	
		BINARY	MULTI-OPTIONAL			
		VOTERS' CHOICE →				

Table 6.7 A party even more divided

Preferences	Ms *i*	Mr *j*	Ms *k*
1st	***A***	***B***	***C***
2nd	***B***	***C***	***D***
3rd	***C***	***D***	***A***
4th	***D***	***A***	***B***

In voting, we get everyone to cast their preferences. Then either we compare every option with every other option, to see which wins the most pairings, (Condorcet or Copeland); or we add up all the points (MBC); or again, we rely on both counts, and if the Condorcet social choice is the same as the MBC social choice, then this will be taken as the true outcome. If there is a discrepancy, then the debate shall be resumed. In a scientific comparison, however, the most accurate measure of a collective opinion is a combined MBC Borda/Condorcet analysis.

Granted, a Condorcet count can suffer from the paradox (para 1.3.1). And a Borda methodology may be vulnerable to the irrelevant alternative, as it is called. If we return to Table 1.6, here repeated as Table 6.7, we see that option ***D*** is actually 'irrelevant' in that all three voters all prefer option ***C***.

In this instance, the MBC scores are ***C*** 9, ***B*** 8, ***A*** 7, ***D*** 6. If the irrelevant ***D*** is removed, the scores are ***A*** 6, ***B*** 6, ***C*** 6. So, with an MBC, add or subtract another option, even an irrelevant one, and the outcome might change.

Yes, the MBC can be subject to an irrelevant alternative, but not a Condorcet/Copeland count. And a Condorcet count can be subject to a paradox and not an MBC. So a combined MBC/Condorcet system is close to perfection.

Reference

Franke, H., & Twitchett, D. (1994). *Cambridge history of China* (Vol. 6). Cambridge: CUP.

Chapter 7
Comparing Electoral Systems

Abstract Comparing the accuracy of various decision-making systems—from binary voting to preferential—is relatively easy, for there can be only one decision. Because elections may cater for the election of one or several candidates, winners and runners-up, overall or in quotas, and so on, there are many more electoral systems, and these vary a lot. Suffice to say that, for any one electorate at any one time with any one set of preferences, a change in the electoral system might cause a *huge* difference in the results. Accordingly, this chapter compares some of the more common electoral systems: the intolerable, the not so bad, the good and two of the best.

7.1 Introduction

There are relatively few decision-making systems but over 300 electoral systems to choose from. As we said in the Preface, some of the former duplicate in either role—plurality voting in decision-making, for example, works in exactly the same way as first-past-the-post FPTP—but needless to say, all the various proportional representation PR systems are used only as electoral systems. Taken altogether, then, electoral systems range from the simplistic and inaccurate Orwellian via the fairer PR systems to the more sophisticated preferential methodologies: from single-preference systems via some multi-candidate voting procedures to those which are both proportional and preferential.[1] We will consider a selection of the more common ones, as well as a relatively unknown but brilliant one.

[1]Invariably in decision-making, the final outcome can be only a sole decision: one social choice, or one prioritisation, whatever, but always a singleton. In contrast, when electing representatives, there may be just the one winner in a presidential contest or in a single-seat constituency in a parliamentary election, or quite a few in a multi-member constituency, as in Ireland's three- or four-seaters, or well over a hundred when the entire country is just the one constituency, as in the Dutch system.

P. Emerson, *Democratic Decision-making*,
SpringerBriefs in Political Science,
https://doi.org/10.1007/978-3-030-52808-9_7

7.1.1 *Orwellian Systems*

Some systems are indeed Orwellian in their simplicity: they ask the electorate to choose just one candidate from a list of many, often ten or more, as if the voter may regard only one candidate as 'good' and by implication all the others as 'no good' if not 'bad'. Such a system cannot give an accurate representation of the individual's wishes; so, the results in such an election are bound to be false. As shown in Tables 7.1, 7.2, 7.3 and 7.4, the various systems range from the simplistic and bad to the more sophisticated and good.

7.1.2 *Two-Tier Systems*

A few systems allow the voter a little more choice: in a two-tier system, as in Germany for example, the voter has two ballots: one is for an FPTP election in a small constituency, and the other is a PR-list contest in a larger region (a Länder); the system is called multi-member proportional, MMP. So, the fan of a big party may vote for the same candidate in both ballots, whereas the supporter of a tiny party may vote tactically in the FPTP constituency because the tiny party doesn't have much chance under FPTP, but it may indeed have a good chance in the PR election.

Table 7.1 Single-ballot electoral systems

Name	Number of candidates	Party political state	PR?	Description The voters:
Majority voting North Korea	1	One-party	X	choose just 1 candidate, whether they like him – it's usually a he – or not.
First-past-the-post FPTP HK, Kenya, India, Malaysia, UK, USA	2 or more but often 2 favourites	Two-party	X	choose just 1 candidate.
Two-round system, TRS France	2 or more	Two-party	X	choose 1 in a plurality vote and, if need be, the same or another 1 in a majority vote play-off.
Single non-transferable vote SNTV Afghanistan	many	n/a[a]	semi	choose just 1 candidate, but in a multi-member constituency.
PR-list closed Israel	many	multi-party	✓	choose just 1 party in a multi-member constituency.
PR-list open Netherlands				choose 1 party or 1 candidate of 1 party in a multi-member constituency.

[a]Afghanistan is one of many examples where the western notion of party politics does not really apply: most Afghani MPs are independents.

Table 7.2 Double-ballot electoral systems

Name		Number of candidates	Party political state	PR?	Description The voters:
Parallel system FPTP or TRS + PR-list Japan, Russia, Taiwan	FPTP	many, 2 favourites	2 big + some small	semi	have two ballots: the first, FPTP, in a small constituency the second, PR, in a larger constituency.
	PR-list	many			
Multi-member proportional, MMP. Germany, New Zealand	FPTP	some favourites	2 big + some small	✓	{The parallel system is semi-PR; MMP is fully PR. In MMP, (but not in a parallel system) the overall result is governed by the PR element.}
	PR-list	many			

7.1.3 Multiple Systems

Other electoral systems give the voters rather more choice, but while they allow the voters to support more than one candidate/party, they do not necessarily encourage them so to vote. In this regard, approval voting is bad, but range voting is even worse. A BC may be just as bad if it is used with an (n, n-1 … 1) or (n-1, n-2 … 0) formula (para 6.3), without allowing for partial voting, but it is preferential so it's in Table 7.4. In Table 7.3 are the non-preferential multi-candidate systems, of which the PR-list systems used in Belgium and Switzerland are more inclusive, especially the latter, allowing as it does for cross-party voting.

Table 7.3 Multi-candidate non-preferential electoral systems

Name	Number of candidates	Party political state	PR?	Description The voters:
Approval voting	many	n/a	X	'approve' of those candidates they consider to be brilliant, good or just OK; and the winner is the one with the most 'approvals'
Range voting	many	n/a	X	have, say, 10 points, each, to divide on many candidates, or to 'plonk' on just one of them.
PR-list open Belgium	many	multi-party	✓	choose 1 or more candidates of 1 party.
PR-list open Switzerland	many	multi-party	✓	choose 1 or more candidates of 1 or more parties.

Table 7.4 Preferential electoral systems

Name	Number of candidates	Party political state	PR?	Description The voters:
Borda count, BC Nauru[a]	some	non-party	X	give a 1, 2, 3... to their 1st, 2nd, 3rd preferences in multi-member constituencies.
Borda count, BC Slovenia[b]	may be many	multi-party		
Modified Borda count, MBC				
Alternative vote, AV. Australia, PNG.[c]	many	A few big, a few small	X	give a 1, 2, 3... to their 1st, 2nd, 3rd preferences in single-seat constituencies.
PR-STV, single transferable vote, Ireland.	many	multi-party	✓	give a 1, 2, 3... to their 1st, 2nd, 3rd preferences in multi-member constituencies
QBS, quota Borda system	many	multi-party	✓	

[a]Nauru has a rather special counting rule: a 1st preference gets 1 point; a 2nd gets 1/2; a 3rd gets 1/3; a 4th 1/4... and so on, which is very clever

[b]The BC is used for the election of Slovenia's ethnic minorities; the main part of their system is PR-list

[c]To be valid, a vote in Papua New Guinea PNG must include at least three preferences: 1st, 2nd and 3rd... which is also very clever; the democratic process crosses the tribal divide

7.1.4 Preferential Systems

Preferential voting systems also allow the voters to be more sophisticated; the best of them may even encourage the voters to be so.

7.2 An Example

Let us now try to compare these electoral systems or most of them anyway. We need, first of all, just one setting: so, let us take a simple example, a democratic nation of just 240 voters, 12 little villages of 20 voters each, and let's imagine that they are preparing to elect a parliament of 10 MPs.

Let it also be assumed

(a) that society is very homogenous—there are no poor ghettoes, rich suburbs, sectarian enclaves or other forms of partisan concentrations of voters of one or other hue;
(b) that every village is the same, politically: 20 voters with 1st preferences for the various parties/candidates—just four of them, ***A***, ***B***, ***C*** and ***D***—as shown in Table 7.5;

Table 7.5 20 voters' 1st preferences

	Number of voters			
	8	3	4	5
1st preference	*A*	*B*	*C*	*D*

Table 7.6 A village profile

Preferences	Number of voters			
	8	3	4	5
1st preference	*A*	*B*	*C*	*D*
2nd preference	*B*	*C*	*B*	*B*
3rd preference	*C*	*D*	*D*	*C*
4th preference	*D*	*A*	*A*	*A*

(c) that every party is frightfully clever and, for each electoral system, they nominate the exact number of candidates—$\boldsymbol{A}_1, \boldsymbol{A}_2 \ldots, \boldsymbol{B}_1, \boldsymbol{B}_2$, etc.—which suit their best interests; and

(d) that every villager is partisan in that they all do just exactly as their parties would want them to.

So no one party has a majority, and an accurate assessment of the 240 voters' collective opinion is again more likely to be achieved by an analysis of the voters' preferences, a full set of which is assumed to be as shown in Table 7.6.

On the face of it, opinions on party/candidate ***A*** are very divided; those on ***D*** are rather less polarised; party/candidate ***C*** enjoys some overall support but, with a 1st or 2nd preference from *every* voter; ***B*** is obviously the most popular. So with 10 MPs to be elected, maybe the fairest result would be something like 2 ***A***, 3 ***B***, 3 ***C***, 2 ***D***. But what happens in practice when different electoral systems are employed?

7.2.1 The Setting

Non-PR systems take place in single-seat constituencies. With PR, the degree of proportionality varies with the 'size' of the multi-member constituency—the number of members to be elected in each; the minimum constituency size is normally taken to be a 3-seater, while the maximum could be anything at all—the Dutch have just the one 150-seater.[2]

[2]To be elected in an Irish 3-seater constituency, a party/candidate will need about 20% support—and this figure is called the threshold; in the Netherlands, it's 0.67%. Every electoral system, then, has its own as it were natural threshold, but some countries impose a legal threshold as well: in Germany, you need 5% to get elected; in Turkey, it's 10%; PR with such a very high threshold is perhaps not very proportional.

The following comparison will examine various electoral systems, either in one 10-seater constituency, and/or in two 5-seaters, as appropriate to the electoral system. The analyses for each electoral system in this hypothetical democracy are shown in Table 7.7.

7.2.2 The Analyses

FPTP First-past-the-post. In FPTP, every constituency should ideally be the same size, i.e. 24 voters, which is one village and a little bit of another. As happens so often with FPTP, there may be endless arguments as to the boundaries of each constituency, as parties/villages seek to gerrymander for their own advantage or prestige. But that may not matter too much in our example of a perfectly integrated democracy.

Once that is all sorted out, the winner is the party/candidate with a plurality of the votes; this might be a majority or, as in this example, it may be only the largest minority: in our single-seat constituencies, the winner is ***A***. Always. So, the analysis is 10 ***A***. FPTP is a horrible system.

TRS Two-round system. TRS is similar, with more of the same gerrymandering. In the vote itself, in every constituency, ***A*** and ***D*** go through to the second round, so the winner is now ***D*** and the full analysis is 10 ***D***. That's pretty horrible too.

AV Alternative vote. With AV, there's gerrymandering again, and the winner is now ***C*** in every constituency—another horror story.

What a nonsense it all is. And it's called democracy? It must be emphasised, however, that the above results for these three systems—FPTP, TRS and AV—would apply only if society was, as hypothesised, homogenous, socially, economically, religiously, ethnically, but not necessarily politically, every village a perfect mix of men and women (and kids) of every race and religion, and every social gathering a mix of different philosophies, in which case, in this example, FPTP, TRS and AV are all hopelessly unsuitable; single-preference PR-list systems are also not the best, especially if conducted in relatively small constituencies. But first...

SNTV Single non-transferable vote. SNTV is a single-preference voting system held in a multi-member constituency. If it was decided to have two 5-seater constituencies, the country could be divided into two, with six villages in each half: so not too much gerrymandering here. In such a 5-seater, the winners could be ***A-D-C-A-B***; so the overall result for two constituencies would be 4 ***A***, 2 ***B***, 2 ***C***, 2 ***D***.

If instead there was just one 10-seater, the overall result would be 4 ***A***, 1 ***B***, 2 ***C***, 3 ***D***.

Parallel In our example of a parallel system, we'll have the more usual combination of FPTP (rather than TRS) and PR-list in a 50/50 system, so 5 MPs are elected by FPTP and 5 in a single-preference PR-list system in the one 5-seater constituency.[3]

So, with FPTP, there are now five constituencies, with 48 voters in each—two villages and a bigger bit: so not quite so many arguments on gerrymandering. The result is 5 ***A***. In a 5-seater PR-list election using the d'Hondt quota or St. Laguë divisor,[4] the result would be 2 ***A***, 1 ***D***, 1 ***C***, 1 ***B***, so the overall result would be 4 ***A***, 1 ***B***, 2 ***C***, 3 ***D***.

MMP Multi-member proportional. With MMP, remember, it's FPTP and PR-list again, but the overall result is determined by the proportionality of the second tier, so the result would be 4 ***A***, 2 ***B***, 2 ***C***, 2 ***D***—or it would be, save for the proviso, as in Germany, that any MP who wins a seat in the FPTP election will be able to retain that seat. That makes our result 5 ***A***, 2 ***B***, 2 ***C***, 2 ***D***, and it also explains why the overall size of the Bundestag varies a little, from one election to the next.

Approval and **Range Voting**. As in decision-making, para 6.3, so too as electoral systems, approval and range voting are very difficult if not impossible to analyse scientifically; they could be conducted in any size of constituency; secondly, they allow the voters to be everything from highly consensual to the complete opposite, totally selfish. Thus, they can cater for the intransigent, as can be found in polarised and majoritarian societies. That said, a version of approval voting is used in village elections in China, a one-party state of course, where there are no elections in towns or cities, let alone in regions or the country at large.

Taking all 1st/2nd/3rd preferences to be 'approvals', a 5-seater would see the election of 2 ***B***, 2 ***C***, 1 ***D***, for an overall result of 4 ***B***, 4 ***C***, 2 ***D***.

A 10-seater analysis would see success for 3 ***B***, 3 ***C***, 2 ***D***, 1 ***A***, with ***B*** and ***C*** tied for the tenth seat, which we'll give to ***B***: so that's 4 ***B***, 3 ***C***, 2 ***D***, 1 ***A***.

---

[3]Some countries use rather odd ratios: Taiwan, for example, elects 73 MPs in FPTP constituencies, and 34 under PR. Overall, therefore, its system is not very proportional at all!

[4]If in a five-seater, parties ***W***, ***X***, ***Y*** and ***Z*** get 40, 24, 20 and 16 votes each, then obviously they should get 2, 1, 1 and 1 seats each. If, however, they get 50, 25, 13 and 12 votes? Umm, now it's not so obvious.

Some systems like d'Hondt (and St. Laguë) use divisors: dividing these seat totals by 1-2-3-4- to get 40-24-20-16, 20-12-10-8, $13\frac{1}{3}$-8-$6\frac{2}{3}$-$5\frac{1}{3}$... and then giving seats to those with the five highest totals, 40–24-20–20-16, which means ***W***, ***X***, ***Y***, ***W*** and ***Z***; so that's 2-1-1–1. (St. Laguë uses 1-3-5-7...).

Other systems, Droop (and Hare), use quotas—footnote 6, para 5.3. When 100 voters elect 5 representatives, the Droop quota is 17; so with 40, 21, 20 and 19 votes, parties ***W***, ***X***, ***Y*** and ***Z*** get 2-1-1-1 quotas... and 2-1-1-1 seats.

There are at least two divisor systems—d'Hondt and St. Laguë, and two types of quotas—Droop and Hare. d'Hondt and Droop tend to favour the bigger parties.

BC/MBC The BC is not PR, and nor for that matter is the more inclusive MBC. If the BC system were used in single-seat constituencies, ***A*** would win them all.

In a 5-seater constituency, party ***A*** could nominate 5 candidates—$A_1 + A_2 + \ldots + A_5$—and thus win all 5 seats, which means 10 overall. The BC therefore, if it's without the rules for partial voting which are so integral to the MBC, can be as bad as FPTP, TRS or AV, or as bad as approval voting—but nothing is as unpredictably unfair as range voting.

If, however, everyone is being 'honest'—as M de Borda wanted them to be—then in a 5-seater, the outcome would be ***B-C-A-D-B***, for an overall result of 2 ***A***, 4 ***B***, 2 ***C***, 2 ***D***.

PR-list Proportional representation-list. Working on the 1st preferences only, which is usually the case, the results in a 5-seater of a d'Hondt or of a St. Laguë analysis would be 2 ***A***, 1 ***B***, 1 ***C***, 1 ***D***, or an overall result of 4 ***A***, 2 ***B***, 2 ***C***, 2 ***D***;
and in a 10-seater analysis by d'Hondt or St. Laguë, it would be 4 ***A***, 1 ***B***, 2 ***C***, 3 ***D***.

PR-STV PR-single transferable vote. Ireland, South and North, uses PR-STV mainly in 3-/4-seater and entirely in 5-/6-seater constituencies, respectively. So potentially, there may be some gerrymandering in the South and rather less up North.

In days long gone, some very large constituencies were fairly common, but the counts therein were often dreadfully complicated, so the maximum in current usage is a 6-seater. In our example, therefore, we consider only two 5-seater constituencies.

So, each constituency of 6 villages has 120 voters, and the quota is 21. If the parties and their voters play their cards 'correctly', this would lead to 2 ***A***, 1 ***D***, 1 ***C*** on the quota, with a big surplus from ***D*** going to ***B***, which was only 3 short of the quota anyway. So, it's 2 ***A***, 1 ***B***, 1 ***C***, 1 ***D*** for an overall result of 4 ***A***, 2 ***B***, 2 ***C***, 2 ***D***.

QBS Quota Borda system. In QBS, we can use either two 5-seaters or, because the maths is so much easier than in PR-STV, one 10-seater constituency.

In a 5-seater, the number of voters is 120, and so the quota is again 21.

The 1st preference scores are ***A*** 48, ***B*** 18, ***C*** 24, ***D*** 30.

There is one 1st/2nd pair: there are 30 ***B*** 1st plus ***C*** 2nd preferences, and 24 ***C*** 1st and ***B*** 2nd preferences, so the ***B/C*** pair get 30 + 24 = a total of 54 of these 1st/2nd preferences, which is well over 2 quotas.

And the MBC scores are ***A*** 44, ***B*** 63, ***C*** 51, ***D*** 42.

In stage (i), ***A*** gets 2 quotas, while both ***C*** and ***D*** get 1 each. So, there is one seat still to be filled.

In stage (ii), the ***B/C*** pair has 54 of these 1st/2nd preferences, which is 2 quotas, but ***C*** already has one person elected, so ***B*** is now added.

So, the final result is ***A*** 2, ***B*** 1, ***C*** 1, ***D*** 1, for an overall result of ***A*** 4, ***B*** 2, ***C*** 2, ***D*** 2, which is also the result of a 10-seater analysis.

Table 7.7 The analyses

Electoral System		Small Constituency/ies				Overall Result			
		A	*B*	*C*	*D*	*A*	*B*	*C*	*D*
A very fair system						2	3	3	2
FPTP	In single-seaters	1	0	0	0	10	0	0	0
TRS		0	0	0	1	0	0	0	10
AV		0	0	1	0	0	0	10	0
SNTV	In two 5-seaters	2	1	1	1	4	2	2	2
	In one 10-seater					4	1	2	3
Parallel voting	FPTP	5	0	0	0				
	+ PR-list	2	1	1	1	7	1	1	1
MMP	FPTP	5	0	0	0				
	+ PR-list	2	1	1	1	5[a]	2	2	2
Approval voting	In two 5-seaters	0	2	2	1	0	4	4	2
	In one 10-seater					1	4	3	2
Range voting	At worst	1	0	0	0	10	0	0	0
BC	In single-seaters	1	0	0	0	10	0	0	0
BC/MBC	In two 5-seaters, maybe	1	2	1	1	2	4	2	2
PR-list d"Hondt	In two 5-seaters	2	1	1	1	4	2	2	2
	In one 10-seater					4	1	2	3
PR-STV	In two 5-seaters	2	1	1	1	4	2	2	2
QBS	In two 5-seaters	2	1	1	1	4	2	2	2
	In one 10-seater					4	2	2	2

[a] As explained above, MMP might mean that, in a 10-seater, more than 10 MPs get elected

7.3 Summary

The fairest system of all, therefore, could be (definitely not the BC, which gives the voter a selfish incentive) but the MBC. The latter, however, is unproportional. So maybe we should opt for either PR-STV in a 5- (or 6)-seater, or QBS in a 5- (or more)-seater. But while 4-2-2-2 is pretty fair, it is not the same as the very fair 2-3-3-2.

Maybe, therefore, another electoral system should be invented, the Borda quota system, BQS, so that the candidates' MBC scores have more significance in the count than their 1st preference tallies. There again, in real life, there are invariably more than just four parties competing, if not a few independents as well. Secondly, many voters do *not* act like ballot fodder—and thank heavens for that! Instead, they cast their preferences as they the voters, and not necessarily as their parties, might wish. So, the chances of most candidates gaining a quota of 1st preferences and being thus elected in stage (i) or (ii) of a QBS election are about as unlikely as it is in a PR-STV election. For the moment, then, the Table 7.8 comparison would suggest that QBS is the best, that or the much more complicated and sometimes, especially if held in small 3-/4-seater constituencies, rather capricious PR-STV.

In many countries, if QBS, PR-STV or any other form of PR had been the norm, the results would have been very different from what actually happened. In the UK general election of December 2019, for example, with nearly 1 million votes, the Green Party won 1 seat; with 17 times as many votes, the Tory Party won not just 17 times, but 365 times as many seats! That's outrageous, you might think. And so do I. The result was, yes, fake.

Indeed, the choice of electoral system is often outrageous: politicians invariably choose that which suits their vested interests. Sadly, human rights lawyers and others

Table 7.8 A comparison

Electoral System		Single or multi preference	As used in elections: Presidential	As used in elections: Parliamentary. Thresholds of PR contests come from the electoral system itself, or from an electoral law. If shown below, they are in brackets.[a]	Classification 1 = terrible 2 = bad 3 = so-so 4 = good: 1	2	3	4
FPTP		single	DRC, USA	Canada, Kenya, India, Singapore, UK, USA (35%)	⊞			
TRS		single	Afghanistan, Brazil, France, Georgia, Russia, Serbia, Senegal, Turkey, Ukraine	France (35%), Iran,[c] Mali Uzbekistan		⊞		
AV		multi	Ireland	Australia, PNG			⊞	
SNTV		single		Afghanistan, Iran,[c] Japan		⊞	⊞	
Parallel	FPTP ½ PR ½	single single		Russia (7%)		⊞		
Parallel	FPTP c.⅔ PR c.⅓	single single		DRC 60/440, Japan 289/176, Mexico 300/200, Pakistan 272/70, Senegal 105/60, Taiwan 73/34		⊞		
Parallel	TRS ½ PR ½	single single		73/77 Georgia (5%)			⊞	
MMP	FPTP PR	single single		Germany (5%) New Zealand			⊞	
Two-tier	PR-list (c) PR-list (c)	single single		South Africa, ½/½ national/regional			⊞	
Approval voting		multi	–	–		⊞	⊞	
BC		multi	Kiribati[b]	Nauru, Slovenia			⊞	
MBC		multi	–	–				
PR-list (closed)		single		Israel, Turkey (10%)		⊞		
PR-list (open)		single		Austria (4%), Bosnia, Brazil, Netherlands (0.67%), Serbia (5%)			⊞	
PR-list		multi		Belgium			⊞	
PR-list		multi		Luxembourg, Switzerland				⊞
PR-STV		multi		Ireland				⊞
QBS		multi		–				⊞

[a]Figures are either from Lijphart 1995, or this author's best guesstimates
[b]A BC was used for choosing the candidates
[c]Some Iranian seats are in single-seat TRS constituencies and others in multi-member SNTV ones

rarely compare the various methodologies' democratic credentials, and nor too do most international election observation missions.[5]

In the above comparison at least, and maybe too in many other voters' profiles, when compared on a scale of accuracy, the fairest electoral system is QBS, ideally, in 5-/6-seater constituencies. Next, as in Table 7.8, comes PR-STV, then, maybe, a BC. After that, it's Denmark's, Germany's and Taiwan's systems, in that order. The rest, as stated, can be and often are hopelessly inaccurate.

7.4 Conclusion

Elections allow the people to 'throw the rascals out' and replace them with a different set of politicians. Better this, of course, than a dictatorship. In many countries, however—in the USA, for example—the chosen methodology of FPTP both in the election itself and in the Electoral College often leads to the politics of the pendulum: in comes Obamacare; next, under Trump, it goes out; then, under a new Democratic Party administration, it might come back in again; later… and so on, ad nauseam. A better electoral system would allow for a more evolutionary process of societal change.

As in Chap. 6 with decision-making systems, so too here, we may now compare the various electoral systems in a two-dimensional display with again, voters' choice on the x-axis and preferences counted on the y-, as in Table 7.9. Here too, reading left-to-right, the x-axis depicts an increasing degree of voters' choice, while the y-axis, bottom-to-top, indicates an increasing number of cast preferences taken into account in the analyses. Yet again, the graph has a natural diagonal, from bad in the bottom left-hand corner, via mediocre in the middle, to accurate in the top-right.

Off the scale altogether lies North Korea: it's 'Candidate ***X***, yes or no?' (as long as it's 'yes'). There's some improvement with a 'Candidate ***X*** or Candidate ***Y***?' type of ballot, if, that is, the choice offered is more than 'Do you want "tweedledum" or "tweedledee"?' Alas, in a two-party electoral system like FPTP, although in theory the voters have a considerable choice, in practice, it often boils down to a choice of two favourites; TRS is not much better.

As far as this book is concerned, single-preference PR systems may also be classified as Orwellian in their simplicity although, if the constituency is big enough—in the Netherlands, as was mentioned, the entire country is regarded as one constituency—a fair degree of proportionality is nevertheless achieved. For the same reasons discussed in para 6.5, approval and range voting are not as good as some of their supporters suggest, and nor too is any form of BC which does not cater for partial voting.

---

[5]From 1986 to 2016, the author has worked as a short- or long-term observer in over 20 elections for the Organization for Security and Co-operation in Europe, OSCE, the first in Bosnia just after the 1992–5 war, the most recent in Mongolia in 2017. The OSCE does not comment on the elephant, the observed country's election system, only on literally everything else.

He has also observed elections and/or referendums in Northern Ireland, Ireland, Russia, Sudan, Scotland and Taiwan.

Table 7.9 Electoral systems

COUNT ↑	CLOSED		SEMI-OPEN		OPEN			
	THRESHOLD		THRESHOLD		THRESHOLD		THRESHOLD	
	High	Low	High	Low	High	Low	High	Low
All preferences							QBS + top-up QBS MBC Condorcet	QBS + top-up
many preferences					AV PNG	PR-list Swiss		
					BC + Approval/Range Voting	BC + Approval/Range Voting	BC + Approval/Range Voting	BC + Approval/Range Voting
some preferences	2-round France		Parallel FPTP + PR Taiwan		AV Australia	PR-list Belgium	PR-STV Ireland	
a few					MMP Germany, New Zealand			
1st preference only	FPTP India, UK, USA	PR-list closed Israel	SNTV Afghanistan	PR- list Poland	FPTP Lebanon			
No preferences DPRK	1 party only		1 candidate of 1 party		1 or some candidates of 1 or some parties		1, some or all candidates of any or all parties	
	VOTERS' CHOICE → →							

Overall, then, preferential voting is essential. As was noted in the same para 6.5, AV is not the best, even though it does encourage some inter-party co-operation; nor for that matter is its PR equivalent, PR-STV, in which co-operation may still play a part although not to the extent which QBS offers. Little wonder then that the top-right corner of Table 7.8 shows that our electoral nirvana is either QBS in lots of 5-/6-seaters or, if it is required to have (some) smaller constituencies, QBS with a regional or national top-up.

Reference

Lijphart, A. (1994). *Electoral systems and party systems*. Oxford: Oxford University Press.

Annex A
The Consensors

A.1 The Ref!

The most difficult job of all, of course, is that of the referees, the chairperson and the consensors. The role of the former is well known; what follows is a summary of the consensors' responsibilities.

Like the chair, so too the consensors, shall be elected, impartial and non-voting. When the former has accepted the motion to be debated and has initiated proceedings in whatever forum and whatever format, the consensors shall:

A.1.1 Prior to the Debate

- set limits to the time (in situ) or length (online) of any contributions (so no more filibusters);
- give guidance as needed to those who wish to propose alternative motions, so to ensure that the latter are in the same format as the original;
- accept all relevant options, as long as (a) these proposals are complete packages and (b) they comply with some agreed norm like the UN Charter on Human Rights;
- formulate a list of all these options; in any in situ gathering, display these options (in summary) on a computer screen;
- both in situ and online, if considered necessary, publish the options in full on a dedicated web-page, highlighting any sections which differ from the original.

P. Emerson, *Democratic Decision-making*,
SpringerBriefs in Political Science,
https://doi.org/10.1007/978-3-030-52808-9

A.1.2 During the Debate

- allow for other options to be proposed and added to the list, subject to a maximum of one proposal per party/participant;
- call the chair's attention to any comment or contribution which they consider to be inaccurate, irrelevant and/or impolite;
- maintain a balanced list of the proposed options;
- if deemed appropriate, suggest that two fairly similar options might be composited; or, for the sake of balance, that another option might be drafted and added;
- if and when requested by the chair, submit a draft multi-option ballot paper; if the topic is complex and/or controversial, the balanced list should usually consist of a minimum of four options and a maximum of six; when it has been agreed to, and…

A.1.3 Prior to the Vote

- announce whether or not the options are listed at random and/or whether they are adjacent to each other on a spectrum[1];
- declare whether or not the outcome of the vote will be binding and, if so, announce the CC threshold for this to be so; and, as implied in Table 3.12, state which consensus coefficients, as shown in Annex C, correspond to which levels of support: 'overwhelming support', 'consensus' and 'best possible compromise'.
- in those debates where it has been possible to arrange the options in a spectrum, publish the interpretations which they will give to all the possible single-peaked combinations of preferences—see Annex B.

A.1.4 After the Vote

- publish and/or display the voters' profile; in a parliament, if and when the debate consists of options which are adjacent, the MPs' single-peaked (or otherwise) curves should also be in the public domain;
- interpret the results, if need be by formulating a composite of the two most popular adjacent options;
- publish the results—every option's MBC score and its CC—and declare the outcome.

---

[1] As a general rule, if the number of options is six or less, the options can be listed in random order; if there are seven or more options, it may be wiser to list the options in sequence. In either setting, the consensors can sometimes regard options as adjacent—para 3.5—and should make this known.

Annex B
Interpreting the Preferences

B.1 The Theory

When the list of options forms a balanced spectrum of adjacent options, then, prior to any vote, it may be necessary for the consensors to inform the voters how each set of preferences will be interpreted.

As was mentioned in para 2.5, in a three-option vote on options ***A-B-C***, there are six possible sets of preferences. If the three options are in a spectrum, four of these sets will be single-peaked: a pair, one from each end

A-B-C, ***C-B-A***

and a couple in the middle

B-C-A and ***B-A-C***.

The other two sets,

A-C-B and ***C-A-B***,

both have two peaks, with a valley in the middle.

With four options to choose from, the choice gets a little larger. At the two extremes, as it were, there are

A-B-C-D and ***D-C-B-A***.

Next, starting with option ***B***, there are the following:

B-A-C-D, ***B-C-A-D*** and ***B-C-D-A***;

P. Emerson, *Democratic Decision-making*,
SpringerBriefs in Political Science,
https://doi.org/10.1007/978-3-030-52808-9

and a similar set of three when starting with option ***C***:

C-A-B-D, ***C-B-A-D*** and ***C-B-D-A***;

so altogether that's 10 sets of preferences.

With five or more options on offer, the choice gets even greater, para 2.5 again, so in these cases—if, of course, the options have been arranged in a spectrum of adjacent options—the consensors should advise the participants how each set of single-peaked preferences is to be interpreted, as follows.

B.2 A Five-Option Ballot

Taking the 40-45-50-55-60% tax rates as our example, ***A-B-C-D-E***, we saw in para 3.4 that someone (like Ms *i*), whose 1st preference is for 60%, will probably have a set of preferences of:

60-55-50-45-40
E-D-C-B-A;

that Mr *j*, whose 1st preference is for 40%, may well vote:

40-45-50-55-60
A-B-C-D-E;

while Ms *k* and Ms *l*, whose 1st preference is for 55%, might choose either:

55-60-50-45-40
D-E-C-B-A,

or

55-50-60-45-40
D-C-E-B-A

respectively; so, Ms *k* may prefer something slightly higher than 55%, while Ms *l* would appear to choose something slightly lower. In like manner, Mr *p* whose 1st preference is for exactly 50% could just cast his 1st preference but, if he knows all too well that partial voting may distort a full interpretation of a ballot, para 4.5.1, and if he wishes to be a good democrat and acknowledges in his ballot the validity of the other options, he could cast his subsequent preferences either side, as it were, in equal measure: either

Table B.1 Sets of preferences and their interpretations

Sets of preferences		Interpretations (%)
40-45-50-55-60	***A-B-C-D-E***	40–2
45-40-50-55-60	***B-A-C-D-E***	43–4
45-50-40-55-60	***B-C-A-D-E***	45
45-50-55-40-60	***B-C-D-A-E***	46
45-50-55-60-40	***B-C-D-E-A***	47
50-45-40-55-60	***C-B-A-D-E***	48
50-45-55-40-60	***C-B-D-A-E***	49
50-45-55-60-40 50-55-45-40-60	***C-B-D-E-A*** ***C-D-B-A-E***	50
50-55-45-60-40	***C-D-B-E-A***	51
50-55-60-45-40	***C-D-E-B-A***	52
55-50-45-40-60	***D-C-B-A-E***	53
55-50-45-60-40	***D-C-B-E-A***	54
55-50-60-45-40	***D-C-E-B-A***	55
55-60-50-45-40	***D-E-C-B-A***	56–7
60-55-50-45-40	***E-D-C-B-A***	58–60

50-55-45-40-60
C-D-B-A-E

or

50-45-55-60-40
C-B-D-E-A.

The full set of preferences and their interpretations are shown in Table B.1: one set of preferences starting with option ***A***, in tint; four with ***B***; six with ***C***, in tint; four with ***D***; and one with ***E***, again in tint. In all, it therefore indicates rather more precision in the centre of the table and rather less at the top and bottom; but, as we said in para 4.5, a collective will is probably 'somewhere in the middle'.

B.3 Partial Voting

As stated in para 3.4.1, if all the individual sets of preferences are all single-peaked full ballots, then so too, the collective will also be single-peaked. It is worth repeating that this may not be the case if some of those voting submit only partial ballots (para 4.5.1). Obviously, if lots of 1st preference-only ballots are submitted, and if they are all in support of, say, option ***D***, then, in the collective will curve of preferences, ***D*** might well be out of 'single-peaked sequence'. If only for this reason, therefore, voters should be encouraged to submit full ballots; but, as in para 4.4, they are anyway, mathematically; experience to date shows that in most instances, most voters submit most of their preferences.

Annex C
Variations of Consensus Coefficients

C.1 The Theory

The maximum CC is always 1.00. The absolute minimum is always 0.00. But the mean and the minimum full ballot levels may vary. In Table 3.12 of para 3.6, here repeated as Table C.1, we saw how different consensus coefficients may be interpreted. And that was for a five-option ballot.

But depending on the number of options, these figures may vary. A full table is as shown in the bottom four rows of Table C.2. The figures for 5- and 10-option columns are shown in bold and tint—these are the authors' assessments for columns

Table C.1 The outcome

The outcome	Consensus coefficients	
	≥	≤
No consensus	–	0.75
Best possible compromise	0.75	0.80
Consensus	0.80	0.90
Overwhelming support	0.90	1.00

Table C.2 Variations on a theme

Description	Number of options							
	3	4	5	6	7	8	9	10
Maximum CC (full ballot)	1.00	1.00	1.00	1.00	1.00	1.00	1.00	1.00
Minimum CC (full ballot)	0.33	0.25	0.20	0.17	0.14	0.13	0.11	0.10
Mean CC (full ballot)	0.67	0.63	0.60	0.59	0.57	0.56	0.55	0.55
Absolute minimum CC	0	0	0	0	0	0	0	0
No consensus	≤0.80	≤0.77	**≤0.75**	≤0.74	≤0.73	≤0.72	≤0.71	**≤0.70**
Best possible compromise	≤0.85	≤0.85	**≤0.80**	≤0.80	≤0.80	≤0.80	≤0.80	**≤0.80**
Consensus	≤0.92	≤0.92	**≤0.90**	≤0.90	≤0.90	≤0.90	≤0.90	**≤0.90**
Overwhelming support	≤1.00	≤1.00	**≤1.00**	≤1.00	≤1.00	≤1.00	≤1.00	**≤1.00**

P. Emerson, *Democratic Decision-making*,
SpringerBriefs in Political Science,
https://doi.org/10.1007/978-3-030-52808-9

in which the maths is all nice round figures. Other figures in these rows are just his best guesses.

As the reader will realise, any partial votes may seriously detract from the final scores. If then the consensors fear, there may be a considerable number of partial votes—and this might be the case in a post-conflict zone, for example—they may choose some lower thresholds. Whatever their decisions, it is of course important for them to make these known, well in advance of the actual start of voting.

Glossary

NB Items marked § are described elsewhere in this glossary. Proper names are emboldened.

Terms enclosed in boxes are those of the author's provenance.

Absolute majority	See majority.
AMS	Additional member system, a partially proportional electoral system based on one vote and two counts, the first under FPTP§, the second, PR-list§; see also MMP.
Approval voting	It can be used in decision-making or in a (non-PR) election. Voters vote for as many options/candidates as they wish; each 'approval' has the same value, and the option/candidate with the most 'approvals' wins.
AV = IRV = PV = STV	The alternative vote can be used in decision-making or in a (non-PR) election. It is a form of preference voting where the voters vote 1, 2, 3… for their 1st/2nd/3rd… preferences. If in the count no option/candidate gets 50% + 1 1st preferences, the least popular option/candidate is eliminated and its votes are transferred according to its 2nd preferences. The process continues until an option/candidate gets or exceeds 50% + 1, or until only one option/candidate remains. See also PR-STV.
BC	Borda count, a points system, can be used in decision-making or in a (non-PR) election, though it is more suitable in the former mode; for its application to a PR§ electoral system, see QBS.

P. Emerson, *Democratic Decision-making*,
SpringerBriefs in Political Science,
https://doi.org/10.1007/978-3-030-52808-9

In a BC of n options/candidates, the voters vote 1, 2, 3… for their 1st/2nd/3rd… preferences, as they wish, up to a maximum of n or, if $N > 10$, a smaller specified number. A 1st preference gets n points, a 2nd preference gets $n-1$ and so on. So (1st/2nd/3rd) preferences get (n, $n-1$ … 1) points, or maybe ($n-1$, $n-2$ … 0). The winner is the option/candidate with the most points. See also MBC.

Binary voting — It can be used in decision-making or in a (non-PR) election, but it's usually used in the former, where a decision is taken in a two-option, for-or-against choice, or in a series of such majority votes.

Binary majority rule — It is the belief in and/or practice of a form of governance in which power in, say, a parliament is exercised by only the bigger 'half' of that parliament—the members of the biggest majority party or those of a majority coalition§—and in which decisions are taken in binary§ votes. See also preferential majority rule.

Binary paradox of voting — or a binary cycle can occur in binary§ or Condorcet§ voting. If there are three or more voters voting on three or more options… if, for example, three voters—Messrs *i*, *j* and *k*—and if Ms *i* has 1st/2nd/3rd preferences of ***A-B-C***, Mr ***j*** has ***B-C-A***, and Ms ***k*** has ***C-A-B***, then in any system of majority voting, and if all vote sincerely, ***A*** will be more popular than ***B***, ***B*** more popular than ***C***, and ***C*** more popular than ***A***. This can be written as: $A > B$, $B > C$ and $C > A$ or

$$A > B > C > A > \ldots$$

and this 'cycle' continues, forever!

Block vote — A (non-PR) electoral system of FPTP§ in multi-member as constituencies where voters may support as many candidates are to be elected.
The term is also used to describe the vote of, for example, trade union delegate, whose single vote may supposedly represent many members.

Borda — See BC.

Borda preferendum — A multi-option vote or referendum conducted under an MBC.§

Citizens' initiative	A mechanism whereby a certain number of citizens can demand a referendum§ on a topic of their own choosing.
Clone	An option which is very similar to another
Coalition	
majority	a union of some parliamentary parties in a government which then commands a simple majority§ in that parliament;
grand	a majority coalition involving the two biggest parties;
all-party	a power-sharing government involving all the main parliamentary parties plus perhaps members of a few others and/or independent members
Composite	An amalgam based on two or more compatible options/policies.
Condorcet	A Condorcet count or pairing vote can be used in decision-making or in a (non-PR) election. The voters cast their 1st/2nd/3rd preferences on the options/candidates, as in AV§. In the count, pairs of options/candidates are examined separately and, in let us say a three-option contest, and if ***A*** is more popular than ***B*** *and* if ***A*** is more popular than ***C***, then ***A*** is the Condorcet winner. See also binary paradox.
Consensor	In consensus§ decision-making, the chair or facilitator is assisted by a team of impartial consensors who monitor the debate in order to then recommend which voting mechanisms if any are to be used, and which options are to be included on any relevant ballot paper.
Consensus	See also consensus coefficient.
verbal	an agreement, sometimes taken after lengthy discussions and after all concerned have agreed to a compromise, without resort to a vote;
'votal'	an agreement, sometimes taken after lengthy discussions, after all have agreed to identify their best compromise via an MBC§ vote.
Consensus coefficient	If S_A is the MBC score of option ***A***, if V is the valid vote and if *n* is the number of options/candidates to be voted on, the consensus coefficient CC of option ***A***, CC_A, $cc_A = S_A / V \cdot n$ That is, an option's consensus coefficient is its MBC score divided by the maximum possible score; it varies from good to bad, from 1.00 to 0.00.
Consensus voting	methodologies, or preferential points voting§ systems, are those in which the winning outcome is that which is most popular amongst everybody; this is not necessarily the will of a simple majority.

Consociationalism	It is a form of government where decisions are taken by simultaneous majorities§ from both or all communities: from both unionist and nationalist (Northern Ireland); from both Czech and Slovak (Czechoslovakia); from all Bosniak, Bosnian Croat and Bosnian Serb (Bosnia); and so on. In effect, every relevant grouping has the power of veto§.
Constituency	Non-PR electoral systems are used in single-seat constituencies, a geographical area represented by just one elected representative. A multi-member constituency has two or more representatives. The word 'constituency' may also be used in a non-geographical sense, to describe a particular group of people who, *inter alia*, relate to one or more representatives.
Cycle	See binary paradox of voting.
Democracy	Rule by the people, *demos*. It can be direct, as it was initially for certain rich males in ancient Greece, or indirect, via a parliament of elected representatives;
consensual	rule by representatives of all the main political parties/opinions, in which decisions are taken in consensus§;
consociational	rule by an all-party coalition§, in which decisions are taken together, as in consociationalism§;
majoritarian	rule by a single party or group of parties which has the support of a majority§ of elected representatives, and in which decisions are taken by majority vote.
D'Hondt	See divisors.
Divisor system	It is a rule of thumb for allocating seats according to party strengths (see also quotas). Every party's vote total is divided by a prescribed set of these divisors to give a series of descending scores. Seats are awarded to the parties with the highest resulting scores, as in the example of footnote 5 to para 7.2.1. Different sets of divisors include the following

d'Hondt	1	2	3	4	....
St. Laguë	1	3	5	7	....
modified St. Laguë	1.4	3	5	7	....

	and each may give marginally different results. d'Hondt tends to favour the relatively larger parties. See also quota.
Droop	See quota.
Electorate	All those eligible to vote.
Filibuster	A long speech, the main purpose of which is to obviate any vote.
FPTP	First-past-the-post, a (non-PR) electoral system where the voter casts one 'x' only. If there are only two candidates, it is a majority vote, and the candidate with a majority§ of

	the votes is the winner. With three or more (a plurality§ of) candidates, the candidate with the most votes wins; in some instances, this winner does not receive an absolute majority of the votes but only the largest minority, a plurality. Thus, FPTP elections with three or more candidates are plurality votes§. So, in a two-candidate contest, a win requires 50% + 1; with three candidates, victory may need only 33% + 1; with 4, 25% + 1... with 10, 10% + 1. It's called FPTP, but there is no P, there is no post.
Franchise	The right to vote in public elections.
Gerrymander	The 'art' of adjusting constituency boundaries so that your own party benefits.
GNU	Government of national unity; see all-party coalition.
Grand coalition	See coalition.
Guillotine	An order to suspend debate and move to the vote.
Hare	See quota.
Hung parliament	It is one in which no one party has an absolute majority§.
Irrelevant alternative	If in a multi-option ballot, with options ***A, B, C, D*** and ***E***, the most popular option is, let us say, ***D***, then ***D*** should still be the most popular option even when an additional but less popular option, an irrelevant alternative like ***F***, or a clone§ like ***B'***, is also included on the ballot.
IRV = AV = PV = STV	Instant run-off voting is the name used in North America for AV/STV. PV is the Australasian term.
Majoritarianism	See binary majority rule.
Majority	(See also coalition)
absolute	50% or more;
consociational	see consociationalism;
qualified	is used in the EU. Depending on their size, different countries have different numbers of votes, and the result depends on certain weightings§;
relative/simple	may be only the biggest minority;
weighted	2/3rds or some such other ratio greater than 1/2.
Majority rule	See binary majority rule.
Majority vote	See FPTP.

Matrix vote	It is a PR§ electoral system by which an electorate can elect a fixed number of persons to be members of a committee or executive of very different positions. It is ideally suited: • for the election of the chairperson, secretary, treasurer, etc., at an association's AGM; and • for a power-sharing administration in which the parliament or assembly elects a all-party coalition cabinet or GNU. The matrix vote is best based on a QBS§ and an MBC§ count.
MBC	Modified Borda count can be used in decision-making or in a (non-PR) election, and is very similar to a BC§. In a ballot of n options/candidates, a voter may cast m preferences, where $n \geq m \geq 1$ points are awarded to (1st/2nd/3rd) preferences cast as per $(n, n-1, \ldots 1)$ *or* $(n-1, n-2, \ldots 0)$ in a BC§ or $(m, m-1, \ldots\ 1)$ in an MBC. If every voter casts a full ballot of all n preferences, a BC§ is the same as an MBC. If some voters submit only partial ballots, however, the difference can be huge. The MBC allows for partial voting§; the BC§ does not.
MMP	Multi-member proportional is a PR§ electoral system based on two votes and two counts, the first by FPTP§ and the second under PR-list§; see also AMS and parallel voting.
Modified St. Laguë	See divisors.
Pairings	See Condorcet.
Paradox	See binary paradox.
Parallel voting	It is a two-part electoral system in which some MPs are elected under one system in small constituencies—usually FPTP or sometimes TRS—while the other MPs are elected under a PR-list system. The ratio is sometimes, but not always, 50:50. It is regarded as semi-proportional; the results of the second PR election have no bearing on the overall results from the first part, which is where parallel voting differs from MMP.§
Partial vote	In a ballot in which the voter is asked to cast (up to) n preferences, a voter may cast m options, where $n \geq m \geq 1$ and, if $m < n$, this is a partial vote. See MBC.
Plebiscite	A referendum,§ possibly on the topic of national sovereignty.

Plural society	It includes two or more different ethnic or religious groups/communities.
Plurality	The largest minority.
Plurality voting	It can be used in decision-making or in a (non-PR) election. It allows the voter to cast only one '*x*'. In an election, it is FPTP§ whenever there are three or more candidates.
Power-sharing	It is a form of governance in which certain ministerial posts may be shared and/or rotated amongst all the major parties and/or independent members.
PR	Proportional representation refers to an electoral system which is designed to ensure party candidates (and sometimes independents) are elected in proportion to the number of votes gained. PR systems are used in multi-member constituencies§ which may be regional—the Länder, as in Germany, or national, the entire country, as in Israel and the Netherlands.
Preferendum	A multi-option referendum. But one of many different counting procedures may be used. A Borda preferendum is an MBC§.
PPV	Preferential points voting is a generic term for the MBC, QBS and the matrix vote. See also consensus voting.
Preferential majority rule	It is a form of governance in which power in, say, a parliament is shared, and in which decisions are taken in preferential MBC§ votes. See also binary majority rule.
PR-list	In PR-list elections, each party 'lists' its candidates in its own order of priority. Seats are awarded to parties on the basis of a divisor or quota system, and if party ***X*** wins *n* seats, then in a closed list system, the first *n* names from the top of the list, or in an open system, the *n* most popular candidates, are deemed elected.
PR-list closed	An electoral system in which the voters vote for one party only.
PR-list open	In the three main types of open PR-list electoral systems, the voter may choose either: one party or one candidate of that party, as in Bosnia; or one or more candidates of one party only, as in Belgium; or one or more candidates of one or more parties, as in Switzerland.

Profile — A voters' profile is their set of 1st and subsequent preferences.

PR-STV — It is based on AV§, though instead of being set at 50% + 1, the quota§ is smaller, depending on the number of persons to be elected. Transfers take place, not only from candidates eliminated, but also from those elected with a surplus over and above that quota. PR-STV constituencies§ usually have from three to six elected representatives.

PV = IRV = AV = STV — Preference voting.

QBS — Quota Borda system is a PR§ electoral system based on an MBC§. The electorate votes by casting preferences, 1, 2, 3... as in PR-STV§. In a multi-member constituency of four representatives, the count consists of two parts, with two stages in each.

If, at any stage, seats are still to be filled, the count proceeds to the next stage.

Part I.

- stage i) any candidate gaining the quota§ is elected;
- stage ii) if any pair of candidates gets two quotas, both are 'elected'.

Part II, in which only unelected candidates are taken into consideration.

- stage iii) any pair of candidates getting one quota is 'elected', the seat going to whichever candidate of the pair has the higher MBC§ score; and finally, if seats are still to be filled;
- stage iv) seats go to those candidates with the higher/highest MBC scores.

Qualified majority — See majority.

Quorum — It is a minimum number or percentage of persons required for a sitting to be regarded as valid.

Quota — In an electoral system, a quota is a specified number of votes which, if attained, ensures the election of the candidate concerned. The most common quotas are the Hare (which is defined as the nearest whole number greater than the valid vote§ divided by the number of seats) and the Droop (which divides the valid vote by the number of seats plus one). Like the d'Hondt divisor§, Droop tends to favour the relatively larger parties.

Quotas can also apply to a minimum number of persons from a specific gender or ethno-religious group.

Referendum — It is usually a two-option but sometimes a multi-option vote by which the electorate may decide a matter of policy. Multi-option referendums can be conducted under the rules of any of a number of methodologies; it's usually TRS§. See also Borda preferendum.

St. Laguë	See divisors.
Serial voting	It is a decision-making voting mechanism in which options are placed in order, let us say from cheap to expensive. A majority vote is taken between the two extremes, and the loser is eliminated; a second vote is taken between the winner and its new extreme opposite; the process continues until there is an overall winner. In theory in serial voting, if people vote sincerely§, the outcome will be the Condorcet§ winner.
Sincere voting	A voter is said to vote sincerely when she votes for those options/candidates in her order of preference, without taking any tactical§ considerations into account.
Single-peaked	A voter's preferences are said to be single-peaked if, when the options are laid out on, say, a big–small, or cheap–expensive axis, or whatever, his 2nd and subsequent preferences lie in descending order to one side and/or the other of his 1st preference.
SNTV	Single non-transferable vote. This semi-proportional electoral system is used in Afghanistan and Japan. The voter casts only a 1st preference, but the constituencies are multi-member.
Sortition	A random selection of individuals; a good sortition is representative from every perspective—racial, geographical, etc.
STV = AV = IRV = PV	The single transferable vote is another name for AV.
Suffrage	See franchise.
Tactical voting	A voter is said to vote tactically (as opposed to sincerely§) if, instead of voting for her preferred option or candidate, she chooses the option or candidate that may result in what she judges to be her best more likely outcome.
Threshold	The threshold of an electoral system is the minimum percentage of votes required for a candidate to be elected; this is usually the logical consequence of the specific mathematics of the electoral system concerned, but there can also be a laid-down minimum of, say, five per cent, as in Germany, 7% in Russia or 10% in Turkey.
Top-up	A top-up is the second part of an election count, applicable to some electoral systems like AMS§, in which votes are counted either in a different way and/or in a bigger constituency, to ensure a greater degree of overall proportionality.
TRS	The two-round system of voting can be used in decision-making or in a (non-PR) election. The first round is a plurality vote§ and, if nothing gains more than 50% support, the second round is a majority vote§ between the two leading options/candidates from the first round.

Turnout	The number of people who, literally, turn out to vote; it is normally expressed as a percentage of the total electorate§.
Two-tier	Electoral system consists of one election (which may be PR§) in small constituencies, and a second election (which is PR) in larger regional or national constituencies. Austria, for example, has a two-tier system based on closed list PR, the Swedish version is open list PR, while Germany's MMP§ consists of two votes, one under FPTP,§ and the other, list PR.§
Valid vote	The number of voters deemed to have handed in a proper, valid vote, be it full or partial.
Veto	The ability to prevent a vote being passed.
Weighted majority	See majority.
Whip	A party whip is either • an instruction from the party leadership to its elected representatives to vote in a certain way; or • the functionary who issues such orders; or • that which is held by those who obey these orders. Those who disobey may well lose this party whip… and thus their careers.
Win-win	A win-win decision is one in which (nearly) everybody wins something but nobody wins everything. It is the opposite of a zero-sum decision.§
Zero-sum	A zero-sum decision places voters in a win-or-lose situation: some win everything, and others lose everything.

Index

NB Items included in the glossary are asterisked

P. Emerson, *Democratic Decision-making*,
SpringerBriefs in Political Science,
https://doi.org/10.1007/978-3-030-52808-9

The manufacturer's authorised representative in the EU is Springer Nature Customer Service Centre GmbH, Europaplatz 3, 69115 Heidelberg, Germany. If you have any concerns regarding our products, please contact ProductSafety@springernature.com

Printed and bound by CPI Group (UK) Ltd, Croydon, CR0 4YY
22/09/2026
02220945-0018